Praise for the Real People, Real F

"Jodie Niznik's writing transcends m. ̄ ̄ ̄
gets actual transformation. . . . With sensitivity and an ongoing
desire to encourage her readers, Jodie introduces each lesson with
a spiritual practice to help them in their relationship with the
Lord."

DR. E. ANDREW MCQUITTY, pastor at large at Irving Bible
Church and author of *The Way to Brave*

"Each weekly lesson includes a practice session to help us apply
gleaned wisdom for navigating our own crossroads. Jodie's studies move us toward transformative biblical literacy and an action-
packed faith that lives what's learned."

SUE EDWARDS, professor at Dallas Theological Seminary and
author of the Discover Together Bible Study series

"Jodie Niznik offers solid teaching and hands-on application
that have the potential to transform us. Filled with outstanding
questions and exercises, [her studies] encourage a deep level of
engagement."

NANCY BEACH, leadership coach with the Slingshot Group and
author of *Gifted to Lead*

"Niznik's highly practical invitations toward spiritual disciplines
further root me in the powerful message that I am loved, God
has a plan for my life, and obedience brings joy. This will be a
perfect Bible study addition to any ministry longing to deepen
women's connection to God."

MARY DEMUTH, author of over forty books, including
Into the Light

"Jodie's Bible studies are some of my favorite resources! Her
insightful and practical application of Scripture keeps her studies
at the top of my list."

KAT ARMSTRONG, preacher, author of *The In-Between Place*,
and cofounder of the Polished Network

REAL PEOPLE, REAL FAITH BIBLE STUDIES

Choose: A Study of Moses for a Life That Matters

*Crossroads: A Study of Esther and Jonah
for Boldly Responding to Your Call*

*Trust: A Study of Joseph for Persevering
Through Life's Challenges*

*Journey: A Study of Peter for Stumbling
Toward Jesus's Extravagant Grace*

A

REAL PEOPLE
REAL FAITH
BIBLE STUDY

JOURNEY

A Study of Peter for Stumbling Toward Jesus's Extravagant Grace

JODIE NIZNIK

KREGEL
PUBLICATIONS

Journey: A Study of Peter for Stumbling Toward Jesus's Extravagant Grace
© 2022 by Jodie Niznik

Published by Kregel Publications, a division of Kregel Inc., 2450 Oak Industrial Dr. NE, Grand Rapids, MI 49505. www.kregel.com.

The image that appears on page 152 was created by Lindsey Sobolik and is used with her permission.

Cataloging-in-Publication Data is available from the Library of Congress.

ISBN 978-0-8254-4736-5, print
ISBN 978-0-8254-7722-5, epub
ISBN 978-0-8254-6873-5, Kindle

Printed in the United States of America
22 23 24 25 26 27 28 29 30 31 / 5 4 3 2 1

To Mom:
I've loved seeing you embrace Jesus and follow
him as his disciple. You remind me a lot of Peter,
and that is a very good thing. Keep being bold and
brave. I'm so proud to be your daughter.

CONTENTS

• • • ● • • •

WHY PETER AND WHY NOW?

•••••••

I've always been drawn to Peter. I love how he seemed so un-inhibited in the way he followed Jesus. One moment he was a fisherman with a boat, a home, and a family—and the next he'd left it all behind to be a penniless student and follower of Jesus. Scripture also paints him with boldness when it recounts the story of Peter asking Jesus to command him to get out of a boat and walk on water. Peter knew that the laws of nature meant he couldn't walk on water, but he believed with Jesus he could—and so he did. He eventually became a bold and brave preacher, gaining the power to heal people in Jesus's name. He was unarguably a powerful man of God.

But Peter was far from perfect. He slept when he should have prayed. He denied Jesus when he should have proudly proclaimed their association. He talked when he should have listened. He even tried to assert his ideas over God's. It's here, in all his flaws, that I identify with Peter the most.

If God can use Peter, who stumbled and fumbled in such dramatic fashion, then he can use me too. This is the extravagant grace of God. He chooses to use us, even with our imperfections.

I've come to believe that this is one of the reasons we get to see Peter's mistakes in Scripture. I think Peter proudly stood by the accounting of his life because he wanted us to know that, just like him, we will all stumble as we follow Jesus, but that's where God's grace comes in.

Every time Peter stumbles as he journeys with Jesus, we see our patient Savior catch him in extravagant grace and set him back on the path of discipleship. Eventually, we'll be witnesses to

Peter as he transforms before our eyes. I hope his journey inspires you as it has me. If Peter can become a powerhouse of God's kingdom, so can we. Peter came to believe that following Jesus was worth it, no matter the cost. I also believe it is worth it. I hope you will come to the same conclusion.

May we stumble toward Jesus together.

—Jodie

WHAT TO EXPECT
IN THIS STUDY

• • ● ● ● • •

Practice Sections

Each week our lesson will start with a short practice section. These practices are an opportunity for you to take some of the concepts we are learning and live them out, perhaps in a way you've never tried before. These practices won't take a lot of time, but they may require some planning. Therefore, we will start each lesson with the practice section. Prayerfully read it through and then make a plan to try the suggested activities.

You may discover something you really love in these little sections—something that brings new life into your relationship with the Lord. You may also discover that some of these exercises will take effort. Some may be hard for you to do and others may be easy, even fun! But they will all help you stretch and grow. Growth almost always brings the spiritual fruit of a changed life. For me, that makes any effort totally worth it.

Pacing Your Study

Each week of this study includes a practice for the week and four study sessions. You are welcome to tackle as much of the week's material as you would like on any given day. However, I suggest giving yourself five days to complete the week's work, and I have marked the sections accordingly. If you break it into these chunks, the study shouldn't take you more than thirty minutes to do each day. If you are a researcher or an extensively reflective thinker, you may want to set aside more time for each day's study time.

In general, you will find the days broken down as follows:

Day one will be reading about and planning for the practice activity.

Days two through five will be Scripture reading and answering the questions in this study guide.

If you start running behind (we all have those weeks), you may have to pick and choose which questions you want to answer. My advice is to make the Scripture reading your first priority. Then if you have time, scan through the questions to see which ones you want to answer.

As is usually the case, the higher the investment, the greater the return. When we collaborate with Jesus by inviting him into our lives and spending time with him, we experience life transformation. As your life is transformed, you will find it looking more and more like the life God designed you to live. Make every effort to arrange your days so that you can regularly spend time with Jesus.

CALLED TO FOLLOW

Day 1
Practice: Lectio Divina

From the first moment Jesus and Peter met, they had a deep connection. Jesus saw who Peter was and who he could become. He knew Peter had the potential to change the world. And he invited Peter to follow him. This calling and invitation was really a way for Peter to get to know Jesus and his ways better. As he followed, he got a front-row seat to Jesus's teaching, healing, and other miracles. He also got to see how Jesus treated people. Peter quickly learned what kinds of people broke Jesus's heart or made him angry. Peter also witnessed how Jesus spent his time and what his priorities were. In short, Peter was invited to become a disciple of his rabbi, Jesus.

Disciple is an ancient word for someone who followed a respected teacher, learned their ways, and committed to living similarly. The closer a disciple followed, the more like their teacher they became. In fact, there was a phrase that many ancient disciples aspired to, which was to be "covered in the dust of their rabbi." As teachers, or rabbis, walked the dusty ancient roads, their disciples would aim to walk so closely behind them and mimic their steps that they would become covered in their rabbi's dust. It's a beautiful picture of what it looks like to follow with intent.

Like us, Peter was invited to a journey like this with Jesus. As we will quickly discover, he had moments when he did follow closely—but also moments when he seemed to veer off course. I think this will become a great comfort to you, as it has been to me, because we can be a lot like Peter. We have moments of getting things right and moments of wandering off.

We obviously won't get to have the same firsthand experiences Peter got with Jesus. Wouldn't it have been amazing to witness one of Jesus's miracles or sit on a hillside and hear him preach in his earthly voice? Thankfully, we do get the details of these events recorded in God's Word. And while we may wish we could have seen Jesus walk the earth like Peter did, Jesus clearly tells us that what we receive is actually better. As believers in Jesus, we get the Holy Spirit. God sent his Spirit to teach, guide, and convict us and ultimately to help us on our own discipleship journey (John 16:7–13). As it turns out, we can still be metaphorically covered in the dust of our rabbi Jesus as we follow him guided by the Spirit.

Since this study is focused on our discipleship journey, I want to introduce you to a few of the ways you can practice being a disciple of Jesus today. Each lesson will start with an activity that is intended to help you grow as a follower of Jesus. Some may be familiar to you—and if so, I hope you will seek to experience them in a fresh way—and some of these practices may be brand new. Either way, I'm hopeful that they will guide you deeper in your discipleship journey. After all, being a disciple isn't just about collecting more information about Jesus; it is also about intentionally following his ways.

This week our practice will be centered on spending time with Jesus through a centuries-old practice called Lectio Divina, which is Latin and simply means the divine or sacred (*divina*) reading of Scripture (*lectio*). This style of reflective reading is a little different from the Bible study methods we use in this study. My hope is that you will find Lectio Divina to be a meaningful addition to how you study God's Word. I've selected a few passages for you to choose from. Each one is an episode that Peter would have witnessed in his first days of following Jesus. Although there isn't space to cover these passages in our lessons, they still hold a lot of insight and truth for us.

> If you would like to experience more Lectio Divina, I encourage you to listen to my podcast, *So Much More: Creating Space for God*, where I read God's Word and guide you through this process. You will also find interviews with Christian leaders on how the Lord guided them in the same passages. You can find the podcast, including a series of episodes that coincide with this study, anywhere you listen to podcasts or on my website, JodieNiznik.com.

I've given you six steps to guide you in this practice and I recommend you set aside at least fifteen to twenty minutes to do it. I'm hopeful that even if the passage you choose is familiar, the Lord will draw you to notice and reflect on something new that helps you know Jesus in a deeper way.

Step One: Relax
Find a quiet space where you can sit in an attentive yet relaxed posture. Take a few deep breaths and ask the Holy Spirit to open your eyes and heart to see what he wants you to see. Ask him to guide you to the passage he wants you to read and reflect on.

Step Two: First Reading
Choose one of the following passages to prayerfully read. This first reading is to familiarize yourself with the text. There is no agenda beyond this.

Passage 1: John 2:12–22, Jesus cleared the temple

Passage 2: John 3:1–21, Jesus taught Nicodemus

Passage 3: John 4:1–27, Jesus interacted with the Samaritan
woman

Step Three: Second Reading and Reflection
Before you begin the second reading of the same text, pray and
ask the Lord to draw your attention to a word or phrase in the
text. Then begin reading the text slowly, perhaps even out loud.
When you are finished reading, sit for a few moments and reflect
on the word or phrase the Lord seemed to draw you to. Try not
to overthink this part. If a word or phrase seems to stand out, go
with it. After you settle on the word or phrase, ask God why he
wanted you to notice this word or phrase.

Step Four: Third Reading and Response
Before you begin the third reading, ask the Lord to help you see
more clearly what he has for you. As you read this third time
notice again the word or phrase from reading two. Feel free to
even stop at the word or phrase and just sit there. Ask the Lord,
how does this apply to my life? (You could explore if there is
something you need to notice, do, say, stop, confess, etc.) Respond
to God in prayer.

Step Five: Fourth Reading and Resting
Read the passage one last time and then take a few moments to
be present with God and rest in his goodness and love for you.

Step Six: Reflect
Take a few minutes to pray or journal about your experience.
Spend time reflecting on whether there is anything God seems to
be inviting you to do, believe, or become as a result of this time
with him. If something comes to mind, write it down. Then write
one next step you could take this week.

PRACTICE REMINDER

If you haven't already, take some time to do the Lectio Divina process with one of the passages listed in the practice section.

Day 2
What Do You Want?

Do you remember the first time you were introduced to Jesus? Maybe you have one of those amazing stories where you've never really known life without him. What a gift. Or maybe you met him as an adult, after living a lot of life without him. This is also a gift in its own way. Perhaps you still haven't quite decided what you think of Jesus. If that's the case, I'm so glad you are doing this study because you will get to see him in an up close and personal way.

For me, I wasn't raised in a Christian home and I had, sadly, lived a lot of life for the tender age of thirteen. That summer I went to camp in the Blue Ridge Mountains and as my cabinmates and I sat around a dying campfire, our counselor told us the story of Jesus and his death and resurrection. She then offered us an opportunity to accept the gift of salvation from him. It was the first time I'd ever heard about Jesus.

I remember each of us scattering about to take time to reflect on what we heard. I lay back on the hard ground and gazed up wide-eyed at the night sky. I'm not sure what was happening with the rest of the girls, but my heart and mind felt like they might explode. Could it be? Did the God of the universe see me and love me? Did he want to give me new life through Jesus, even after all the terrible things I had done? My counselor assured me that was the case. She then invited me to imagine that Jesus was offering me a gift and if I wanted it, I could take it.

I can still vividly picture what I imagined that night. It was a huge gold box with a big white bow. (That feels like a heavenly gift, doesn't it?) I told Jesus I believed in him and received his gift. When I opened the box, light poured out. In that moment, I was forever changed. I still knew very little about God or Jesus; I just knew I felt loved, seen, and known in a way I had never felt before. I felt like a weight had been lifted off my young shoulders.

A few years later, when I was nineteen, I felt another call. This time it was an invitation to follow Jesus in a deeper way. You see, since I had entered college, I had been trying to live life on my own terms, and I was not doing a great job. As I was crying out to him for help, he made it clear that I needed to change some things. This invitation wasn't as easy and seemingly beautiful as the first one. It felt scary and hard. It meant changing friends. It meant disrupting my lifestyle. However, my way clearly wasn't working, and I had a deep sense that even though his way would feel initially disruptive, following Jesus intentionally would ultimately lead me to deeper joy and peace.

As we embark on our study of Peter, we will see that he also had multiple callings. The apostle's initial call to follow Jesus was just a first encounter. It was the beginning of Peter getting to know Jesus. Later Jesus called Peter again, and this time asked him to leave everything and follow him.

Peter's faith journey is much like our own. He took steps forward and backward with Jesus. I love that Scripture doesn't scrub out his missteps to only highlight the bright spots of Peter's life. Instead, his highs and lows shine together and reveal Jesus's extravagant grace for Peter . . . and us.

Wherever you are on your faith journey, know that Jesus is calling you to take another step toward him. My prayer is that this study will help you take those next steps—even if they feel a little scary and hard. Because the way of following Jesus is always the better way.

Read John 1:35–42.

A number of people are mentioned in this passage. It can get confusing fast. And to make it even more confusing, one person can be referred to by multiple names. Just like I could be called "Niznik," or "Jodie," or even "Jodie Gail." All are suitable names for me. (But please don't call me Jodie Gail or I'll think I'm in trouble.) Sometimes several people have the same name or similar names. (How many Jennifers do you know?) Thus, before we get started, let me give you a little cheat sheet on who we will be studying.

John the Baptist

John, also known as John the Baptist (Matthew 3:1), was the one God sent to prepare the way for Jesus. He said of himself, "I am the voice of one calling in the wilderness, 'Make straight the way for the Lord'" (John 1:23).

Andrew and John the Apostle

John the Baptist's two disciples, or students, were Andrew (John 1:40) and most likely John the Apostle. We presume the unnamed disciple is John the Apostle because he became the author of the book of John. John was a common name, and this is why we differentiate the two men with distinctions of John the *Apostle* and John the *Baptist.*

Peter

Peter is our main character. He is called Simon, Simon Peter, Peter, and Cephas (Greek for Peter) throughout Scripture. He was given the name Simon Bar-Jonah at birth (Matthew 16:17 ESV). Bar-Jonah simply means "son of Jonah." Today we might call him Simon Jonahson. Simon was a very common name. There are at least seven different Simons in the Gospel accounts and Jesus had two disciples named Simon (Simon Peter and Simon the Zealot). Jesus gave our Simon the name Peter.

Simon Peter was originally from Bethsaida (John 1:44) but moved to the larger town of Capernaum (Mark 1:21, 29) before he met Jesus. Both towns were located on the northern side of the Sea of Galilee. Simon Peter was a fisherman by trade and owned his own boat, indicating he may have had some level of success in the business. He was also married. We know this because Jesus healed Simon Peter's mother-in-law in Luke 4:38 and Paul states in 1 Corinthians 9:5 that Simon Peter took his wife on at least one missionary journey.

Simon Peter became the leader of the original twelve disciples of Jesus, also sometimes called the apostles, and he is mentioned by name more than anyone else (besides Jesus) in the Gospels. He was clearly important to Jesus.

1. John the Baptist saw Jesus passing by and pointed him out to his disciples. The two set out after Jesus. What did Jesus say to them in John 1:38 when he spots them?

2. As you embark on this Bible study journey of following after Jesus through the eyes of Peter, imagine Jesus turns and asks you, "What do you want?" or "What are you seeking?" (John 1:38 ESV). Take a moment to pray through this question. How would you honestly respond to Jesus? (Do your best not to give a "churchy" or pat answer, but to state what you truly want.)

3. Andrew and John followed Jesus and spent the day with him. Andrew couldn't keep Jesus to himself. Read the following verses and circle the three actions Andrew took next.

"The first thing Andrew did was to find his brother Simon and tell him, 'We have found the Messiah' (that is, the Christ). And he brought him to Jesus." (John 1:41–42)

I want to make sure you clearly see the three things Andrew did. So, while I won't do this a lot, I am going to answer the previous question for you. Andrew *found* his brother, *told* him about Jesus, and then *brought* him to Jesus.

4. Has anyone ever done something like this for you? What happened? Why was it effective or ineffective?

5. Pray and ask God if there is anyone he wants you to find, tell, and bring to him. If someone comes to mind, ask the Lord to help you think of some practical ways you could do this and write them below. What steps can you take this week to start this process? Is there anything that feels like it is holding you back? If so, what is it?

If you feel like God is asking you to find, tell, and bring someone to him in some way, remember that you're only responsible for this piece. It's the Holy Spirit's job to manage the outcome and change hearts. I know that in today's world, it may feel a little unnerving to tell people about Jesus. If you feel this way, I want to encourage you to start by sharing your story. Tell about how Jesus has helped you, comforted you, met you, or changed you. Sharing your story with another person is almost always welcomed. Finally, as one last source of encouragement, don't forget that sharing Jesus with another person is an extraordinary act of love. If they choose to accept his invitation, their life will be forever better for meeting him.

After Andrew brought Simon to Jesus, Simon's life was forever changed. To signify this change, he was given a new name.

Naming is significant in Scripture. New names signify a new identity. God renamed Abram to Abraham (Genesis 17:5) to signify that Abraham would be the "father of many." A few verses later God changed the name of Abraham's wife, Sarai, to Sarah to signify that she would be the mother of many nations (Genesis 17:15–16). In Genesis 35, God renamed Jacob to Israel to signify that a nation will come from him. And here Simon is renamed to Cephas, which is Aramaic, and when translated to Greek becomes Peter. Both Peter and Cephas mean *rock*.

> 6. Knowing that naming signifies a new identity, what do you think Jesus was communicating to Peter about who he would become? (See also Matthew 16:18.)

"We all have names; but each name is exclusive to each of us. We're named, not numbered, at our birth and baptism. Naming is honoring. Naming is choosing."[1]

—Eugene Peterson

This is one of my favorite moments in Peter's life. Peter met Jesus for the very first time and Jesus told him who he was, "You are Simon son of John" and then told him who he would become, "You will be called Cephas" (John 1:42). He essentially said "You are common" and "You will be a rock." I deeply love this about Jesus—just like with Peter, he sees who we are and who we will be. So, who will you be? Ask Jesus to help you follow him so you can fully become the person you should be, just like Peter did.

If you haven't already, take some time to do the Lectio Divina process with one of the passages listed in the practice section.

Day 3
Miracles and Other Lessons

Read John 2:1–11.

Just before this passage (John 1:43–51) we learn that Jesus also called Philip and Nathanael to become disciples. These two were added to the original three—Simon Peter, Andrew, and John the Apostle—and brought the total to five disciples.

These five men followed Jesus and began to learn from him. They traveled together to Cana in Galilee and attended a wedding. It's hard for us to understand, but when the wedding host ran out of wine, it was a serious faux pas and would have reflected very poorly upon the family. Jesus's mother, Mary, came to Jesus with the problem. Jesus at first seemed resistant to helping, but then did help and with extravagance. This is Jesus's first recorded miracle—turning water into wine.

"Why would this be the inaugural act? Why would Jesus, to convey what he had come to do, choose to turn 150 gallons of water into superb wine in order to keep a party going? The answer is that Jesus came to bring festival joy. He is the real, the true 'Master of the Banquet,' the Lord of the Feast."[2]

—Timothy Keller

7. In the verse below circle what Jesus revealed through the miracle. Underline the result.

"This miraculous sign at Cana in Galilee was the first time Jesus revealed his glory. And his disciples believed in him." (John 2:11 NLT)

What do you think it means that Jesus's glory was revealed?

8. Pause for a moment and imagine what witnessing this miracle might have been like. Remember, you've never seen anything like this before. If you were Peter, what might you have been thinking about Jesus?

As we will discover, the disciples did believe in Jesus, and yet they did not *fully* understand who he was. They were just starting their discipleship journey and with it the discovery of who Jesus was and what he had come to do.

9. Have you ever witnessed something that felt like a miracle to you? If so, what happened? Is it hard for you to call this thing a miracle? Why or why not?

10. Think back to the first time you believed in Jesus. What was it that made you believe? How has your understanding of Jesus changed as you've gotten to know him more? If you don't yet believe that Jesus is God's Son sent to save us, what do you think of him right now? What questions or hesitations do you have about him?

11. In our practice section I listed three passages that we wouldn't be able to cover thoroughly. These are three additional episodes that Peter and the other new disciples got to experience with Jesus. Each taught them something more about the man they were following. Next to the passage you read and reflected on, write what you think Peter learned about Jesus. If you have time, choose one additional passage to read, and write what you think Peter learned.

Passage 1: John 2:12–22, Jesus cleared the temple

Passage 2: John 3:1–21, Jesus taught Nicodemus

Passage 3: John 4:1–27, Jesus interacted with the Samaritan woman

If you haven't already, take some time to do the Lectio Divina process with one of the passages listed in the practice section.

Day 4
Leave Everything Behind

Read Luke 5:1–11.

Piecing together the Gospel accounts can get a little tricky. Each of the four Gospel writers (Matthew, Mark, Luke, and John) told the Gospel story from a slightly different perspective and thus emphasized different aspects of the story. They also followed their cultural norms of storytelling, which doesn't value chronological order nearly as much as our culture does. Nevertheless, the Gospel stories, while sometimes hard to put in exact order, are still the inerrant Word of God inspired by the Holy Spirit. This means that when we run up against something that seems contradictory, it is a good idea to do a little more research to try to understand what is really happening.

With this in mind, if you read the calling accounts in each of the four Gospels (Matthew 4:18–20; Mark 1:16–18; Luke 5:1–11; and John 1:40–42), you will notice that there are two distinctly different stories about Peter's calling. How do we reconcile these very different accounts? I think the best way is to understand that Peter was invited to follow Jesus two different times. The first calling, which we read about in the beginning of this lesson (John 1:40–42), led Peter and the others to follow Jesus for a short time. Peter then seemed to return to his regular life as a fisherman and husband. Scholars think it was about a year later when Jesus saw Peter and his brother Andrew fishing and called them again to follow him.

12. Using the dialogue boxes below, retell what each person said (or what you think they would have said) in your own words based on Luke 5:1–11.

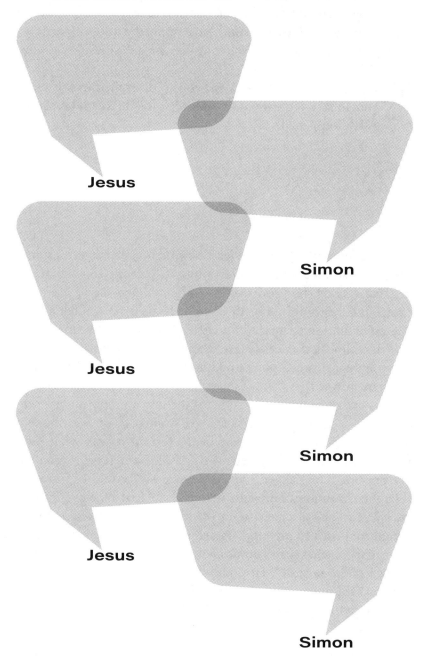

Jesus

Simon

Jesus

Simon

Jesus

Simon

In this account we learn that Peter had worked hard fishing all night and returned empty-handed. By fishing at night, Peter was following the best fishing practices of his time. When Jesus asked Peter to go against this best practice and take the boat into deep water during the day, it would have seemed a foolish waste of energy. And yet, tired as I'm sure he was, he did as Jesus told him.

13. Have you ever felt God ask you to do something or place you in a circumstance that didn't seem to make sense? What happened?

Multiple times in my life I've felt like God invited me to do something that seemed a bit counterintuitive. Recently this happened in a big way as the Lord seemed to be nudging me to leave my career and pastoral role at my church. To be honest, it felt a little like an invitation to jump off a cliff. This is a role I've loved and held for almost thirteen years. Feeling the prompting to move away felt confusing—plus, I had no idea what he might want to move me toward.

This nudge from the Spirit thrust me into a pretty intense season of discernment. The last thing I wanted to do was make a life-changing decision without being certain it was what God wanted. In this season, I spent a lot of extra time journaling my prayers. This helped me slow down so I could capture my thoughts, questions, and fears in one place. It also helped me create space to be still and listen to God. Over the weeks, as I read my journal back to myself, I started to see patterns emerging that seemed like little arrows pointing me to make this move. Another thing I did was seek wise counsel from people who know and love Jesus and me. At every turn I was receiving confirmation that it was time for me to make the shift.

This process took me quite some time to move through. And even when I knew it was the right thing to do, it still felt like a huge leap of faith.

As I write this, the move is still fresh for me. God has been gentle and kind to me in this season of invitation to a new unknown. I want to encourage you that if God is nudging you, take some space to really reflect and discern what he seems to be saying. And if all signs seem to point to him wanting you to make a change, then take the leap of faith. While I don't know how my story ends quite yet, I feel the peace of God surrounding me as I've stepped out in faith to follow his lead.

14. What two responses did Peter have after he caught such a large number of fish (Luke 5:8–9)? Why do you think he wanted Jesus to go away from him?

Through this miraculous catch of fish, Peter caught a glimpse of Jesus's holiness, and in that moment became acutely aware of how sinful he truly was. It's important to pause here and note that Jesus called Peter to follow him while Peter was still a sinner. He does the same for us. We are not called to clean ourselves up before we start following Jesus. The idea that we could make ourselves presentable to God before we come to faith is theologically inaccurate, anyway. Scripture is clear that Jesus died for us while we were still sinners (Romans 5:8) and the only way we are made right in God's sight is through our faith in Jesus (Romans 3:23–24; Ephesians 2:8–9). When we begin to grasp just how much Jesus gave for us, we will find ourselves responding like Peter did at the end of this experience.

15. In the end, what did Peter do as a result of this encounter with Jesus (Luke 5:11)? Do you really think he left everything? Why or why not?

16. When you first became a follower of Jesus, was there anything that you had to leave behind so you could follow him? If so, what?

17. Is there anything you feel like you need to leave behind so you can follow Jesus more intentionally today? Take a moment to pray and ask God to show you if there is anything he wants you to change or give up. If something comes to mind, capture it below. If it's a big change, seek out a wise Christian friend who will intentionally pray with you about this.

PRACTICE REMINDER

If you haven't already, take some time to do the Lectio Divina process with one of the passages listed in the practice section.

Day 5
Different Priorities

Read Mark 1:21–39.

Today we are going to shift our focus to the Gospel of Mark to discover one of the first and most important lessons Jesus taught Peter. This lesson will come up again and again.

In this passage Jesus was with his disciples Peter (who is called Simon in this passage), Andrew, James, and John the Apostle. They went to Capernaum where Jesus entered the synagogue and began to teach.

The Gospel of Mark was written by John Mark, who was close to Peter. Most Bible scholars believe that John Mark wrote the book based on Peter's preaching. Because of this it is sometimes considered Peter's Gospel.

. . . .

18. Fill in the table below based on the verses.

Verse	Location	What Jesus Did	Response of the People
Mark 1:21–22	Synagogue in Capernaum	Taught	Amazed because he taught with authority
Mark 1:23–28			
Mark 1:29–31			
Mark 1:32–34			No response is recorded

All of these events seemed to happen on the same day. It was early on the Sabbath when they went to the synagogue, and then once the sun had set and the Sabbath was officially over, Mark tells us that the people brought the sick and demon possessed for healing (Mark 1:32–34). Since people didn't arrive before nightfall, it's safe to assume it was a long and late night for Jesus, the disciples, and Peter's entire household.

The next morning Peter woke up and couldn't find Jesus. Peter finally found Jesus, alone and in prayer.

19. Why do you think Jesus went to pray? What were some things he had to put aside so he could spend this time alone in prayer? (Consider what's implied in the text, but also what you think.)

Scripture tells us that Jesus frequently retreated to be alone and pray. Some of the times we see him do this are in Mark 6:46, 14:32–38; and Luke 5:15–16.

20. Take an honest inventory of your prayer life over the last few weeks. What are some things that tend to distract you from prayer? Brainstorm and write down a few practical things you could do that would help you keep prayer as a priority in your life. Choose one and make a plan to try it over the next few days.

I've heard the question, "Why did Jesus, who was fully God and fully man, need to pray?" It's an interesting question. After all, since he is God, wouldn't it be like he's just talking to himself? Well, not really. Philippians 2:5–11 tells us that when Jesus became a man, he humbled himself and took on a human form. This means that he had to learn how to live in obedience to God as a human being, just like we do. When Jesus prayed, he was spending time with his Father, God. He was seeking his will, being encouraged, strengthened, guided—and so much more. I think the bottom line for us is that if Jesus needed this time with the Father, how much more do we?

When Simon Peter finally found Jesus he exclaimed, "Everyone is looking for you!" (Mark 1:37). Given the activities of the previous night, it seemed word had spread around town and more people wanted healing. Simon Peter appeared to think this was reasonable and expected Jesus to come back and continue his healing ministry. But Jesus had different plans.

21. How did Jesus respond to Simon Peter (Mark 1:38)? Why do you think Jesus wanted to preach instead of physically heal? How do you think his time in prayer affected his decision and response to Simon Peter?

22. At the end of each lesson, I will invite you to capture the main lessons you think Peter may have learned about what it meant to be a disciple. I want to encourage you not to overthink this. There are no exact right answers. In fact, many weeks will have multiple answers. The intention is for you to look back over the weekly questions and ask yourself what you think Peter learned. If you're doing this study in a group, I hope you will be encouraged by both the variety of answers and the underlying similarities.

So, let's give it a try. The main discipleship lessons I think Peter learned were:

Now, I'd like to ask you to prayerfully consider what you think the Lord wants you to remember most from this lesson. Flip back through this week's questions, including the practice section, and see what the Lord helps you notice. Ask yourself questions like: Did I learn something new? Do I feel like God is inviting me to trust or follow him in a new way? Is there a change I need to make? Or is there something else he seems to be drawing my attention to? Capture your thoughts here.

My takeaways are:

PRACTICE REFLECTION

1. Look back over the passage you reflected on in the practice section. What was doing Lectio Divina like for you?

2. Did you learn anything new about yourself or God through this activity? If so, what?

3. Do you feel like God wanted you to do anything differently as a result of reading and reflecting upon his Word? If so, what?

LEARNING TO FOLLOW

Day 1

Practice: Worshipping Through Song

My grandmother died at the age of ninety-six and thankfully she was mostly healthy until the last year of her life. That last year of pain and weakness was awful, though. I watched as her body seemed to betray her daily. I have a vivid memory of one of my last nights with her. I sat by her bedside while she slept peacefully. The room felt eerily quiet as a gentle Michigan snow piled up on the corner of her windowsill. That moment held peace but also deep pain and confusion. Tears filled my eyes as I silently questioned God. Why would he allow so much pain and suffering? In that moment, it just didn't make sense. I didn't get any answers that night. God felt so far away, and yet in hindsight I can see how near he was.

A few weeks later I was back home in Texas and at church. We started singing a worship song that nearly leveled me. As I sang truth about God's goodness, his nearness even when he felt far away and the fact that he would never abandon me, my soul started to remember what was true of God. In his holy yet gentle way, God was reminding me that even though I didn't understand all the whys of the situation, he was still good, still very much in control, and he would not forsake me. And even more importantly he would not forsake my grandmother. She passed away a few weeks later. I rest in the truth that she is in his presence fully healed.

⚜

If you are wrestling with questions that don't seem to make sense in your own life, Google "Not for a Moment" by Meredith Andrews and listen to this beautiful song for free on YouTube or another similar site. This was the worship song I sang that morning. I pray it will be as helpful to you as it was to me.

Looking back, it's obvious that worship helped redirect my questioning heart back toward God. As I recited truth, my soul was realigned to who he is and what he is about. This is one of the reasons I believe we are called to worship God as a part of being his disciples. The world can weigh down our hearts, easily distracting and deceiving us. Worship reminds us what is true and right and moves our burden back to the only one capable of holding it—our loving God.

I've experienced the power of worship multiple times. In fact, when I start to get bogged down with worry, fear, or questions, listening to and singing along with worship music changes my perspective. As I recite familiar words of truth, I feel my heart and soul shift away from what seems to be plaguing me and back toward hope and faith in God.

Although worship can and should happen outside of just singing to God (for example, reading Scripture, walking in nature and appreciating it, serving others, etc.) worshipping through song is what we are going to focus our practice on. Perhaps you think immediately of the worship music set during church. This is an amazing time to worship God, but we can also sing praise to God privately in our daily lives.

This week I want us to be intentional and choose to worship through singing both corporately and privately. For corporate worship your goal is to be fully present and engaged for your church's *entire* worship service. If for some reason you are unable to be physically present at your church this week, decide how you can be intentional as you watch online. For example, you could stand and sing aloud during the worship time. If you are able to be physically present, commit to showing up a few minutes early to get settled before the service starts. For private worship, choose to set aside time every day this week to engage intentionally with worship music. You could do this by listening to a favorite song before you start your Bible study time, singing while you are driving, or even humming along to worship music while you are doing tasks around the house.

My hope is that as you participate in the practice of intentional worship you will remind your heart of who God is. And then this will draw you to trust him, no matter the circumstances you find yourself in.

In some ways, this is what we observe happening in Peter's life. This week we will read about how Peter witnessed healing, made significant sacrifices to follow Jesus, and chose to take a bold step of faith and trust. All of these things were acts of worship. And while we don't frequently see Peter singing hymns and songs, we do know that he regularly sang psalms of praise as a part of being a Jewish man who practiced his faith (Matthew 26:30). No matter how you look at it, Peter was discovering who Jesus was and this, combined with who he knew God to be from his Jewish heritage, resulted in his faith muscles being strengthened. We may not get the same opportunities Peter did, but through worship we can build up our own faith muscles. And then when the moment comes for us to trust God in new ways, we will be ready.

Set aside time to listen to and engage with
worship music today. Also, plan for how you will
be intentional with your Sunday worship time.

Day 2
Inconvenience and Sacrifice

Read Mark 2:1–12.

In this passage the disciples headed back to Capernaum after a
few long days of preaching and healing. Word had spread about
Jesus and, as a result, more and more people wanted to see him—
either for their own healing or to see if what people were saying
was true.

The text tells us that the people heard Jesus had come "home"
(Mark 2:1). Capernaum was where Peter lived, and Scripture
indicates Jesus didn't have a permanent residence (Luke 9:58).
Thus, while it isn't stated outright, it is logical to assume that
the home referred to is actually Simon Peter's home. It may have
been referred to as Jesus's home because whenever they were
in Capernaum that is where Jesus would stay. A little like the
Spanish saying, "Mi casa es su casa," which means, "My home is
your home." Peter's home was considered Jesus's home.

1. What do you think Simon Peter's family thought of Jesus? (Also see Mark 1:30–31.) Assuming this was Simon Peter's home, how do you think they reacted to all the people and the possible damage to their property? How do you think you would have felt if this was your home?

2. According to verse 5, how did Jesus initially heal the paralyzed man? Why was this (verse 10)? Compare this answer to how Jesus responded to Peter in Mark 1:35–39. (We looked at this passage on day 5 of lesson 1.) Do you see a pattern in what the people wanted from Jesus versus what Jesus wanted to do for them? Why do you think there was a difference? How do you see this same thing happening today in what people hope for or want from Jesus?

3. What did the teachers of the law think about Jesus's forgiveness of the man's sins? How did Jesus know what they were thinking, and how did he respond? What do you think the teachers of the law thought or felt when Jesus called them out in this way?

4. Jesus also healed the man physically. What was the response of the people (verse 12)? Do you think they understood what had really happened?

The call to follow Jesus is often messy and inconvenient. Peter and his family paid a high price for Peter to follow Jesus. Not only was Peter gone for much of the time and unable to maintain his fishing business, when he did come home, he brought crowds with him. There were extra mouths to feed, and in this case, there was likely physical damage to the home.

5. Think back on your journey of following Jesus. What kinds of sacrifices have you made? Is there a time that stands out to you when you felt that you were asked to pay a high cost to follow Jesus? If you paid this cost, was it worth it? If you didn't, do you regret not doing so? Why or why not?

As Peter continued his journey with Jesus, more disciples were added to the group. After a night of prayer, Jesus chose twelve men from the group of disciples and designated them as apostles. He then gave them authority to preach and drive out demons. Scripture refers to this group as the disciples, the twelve, and the apostles. From this point on in the story, when one of these terms is mentioned, unless told otherwise, we can assume that it is the twelve apostles who are being referred to. Their names are listed four times in Scripture (Matthew 10:2–4; Mark 3:16–19; Luke 6:14–16; and Acts 1:13), and each time the order varies slightly as does the names they are called by. However, Peter is always listed first. This, along with the rest of what we know about Peter, leads us to believe that Peter served as the primary leader of the apostles.

The term *apostle* simply means "one who is sent." There were twelve original disciples, and later Judas's replacement and Paul, whom Jesus selected and to whom he gave this official office. Many still use the term *apostle* to mean someone who is sent to minister on behalf of Jesus, but in Scripture the term is mostly used for this select group of men.

••••••

Set aside time to listen to and engage with
worship music today. Also, plan for how you will
be intentional with your Sunday worship time.

Day 3
Take Courage

Read Matthew 14:22–33.

Peter had two main experiences that lead into the passage we are
studying over the next few days. The first is that Jesus gave him
and the rest of the apostles hands-on ministry experience by sending them out in groups of two to drive out evil spirits and heal
disease and sickness (Matthew 10). When the apostles returned,
they were no doubt tired yet exhilarated, and they desired time
with Jesus to process what they had experienced—both the suc-
cesses and the failures. Unfortunately, it doesn't seem like they
got this space as the rigors of ministry kept coming.

The second experience was when Jesus and the twelve set off
in a boat to find a quiet place to rest and reflect. It was a perfect
plan—if it wasn't for all the people. The crowds recognized Jesus
in the boat, and they ran ahead to meet him at the shore. By the
time Jesus and his apostles docked there were at least ten thousand desperate, longing, hurting, and broken people gathered.

Scripture tells us there were five thousand men present
(Matthew 14:21), which means it could have been anywhere
between ten thousand and twenty thousand when you include
women and children.

········

Jesus felt deep compassion for the people. But it was getting late, the location was somewhat remote, and the people were getting hungry. The disciples recommended that Jesus send the people away so they could go get food, but Jesus had other plans. He told the disciples that they should feed the crowd. A quick assessment of their resources revealed that they had only five loaves and two fish. It would take a miracle to feed all those people with what amounted to a small lunch for one . . . but that's exactly what happened. Jesus multiplied the food and fed everyone there. Every. Single. One. They even had leftovers. This meal, while a miracle of Jesus's, still took real work on the part of his disciples. Jesus provided the food, but the disciples provided the service. They shuttled food back and forth for thousands of people and then collected all the extra. They were tired to begin with; now they had to be flat-out exhausted. If you have time, read this story in Matthew 14:13–21.

These two experiences set the stage for one of Peter's most famous interactions with Jesus, walking on water.

6. Look closely at Matthew 14:22–23 (in the sidebar). Does it appear Peter and the others wanted to get on the boat? Why do you think this is? Using your imagination, write out what you think the disciples might have said to Jesus about getting on the boat without him.

"Immediately Jesus made the disciples get into the boat and go on ahead of him to the other side, while he dismissed the crowd. After he had dismissed them, he went up on a mountainside by himself to pray."
—Matthew 14:22–23

The disciples seemed reluctant to get on the boat. It didn't make sense to them to leave Jesus behind, but he was insistent and so they went. By doing what Jesus told them to do they were acting in trust and obedience. Yet that night a strong wind kicked up and the waves of a storm came upon them. Even though they had done exactly what Jesus told them to do, they were not protected from the storm.

7. Thinking back over your journey with Jesus, have you ever acted in obedience but still experienced storms in your life? Do you think the storms would have come regardless of your actions? What did you learn as a result of your storms in the midst of obedience?

"As we read our Bibles, we discover that there are two kinds of storms: storms of *correction*, when God disciplines us; and storms of *perfection*, when God helps us to grow. Jonah was in a storm because he disobeyed God and had to be corrected. The disciples were in a storm because they obeyed Christ and had to be perfected."[1]

—Warren Wiersbe

8. What did Jesus do after he dismissed the crowd? What detail does John 6:15 add to the story for why Jesus wanted to be alone? Why do you think he didn't want to allow the people to have their way?

9. Describe or draw what the disciples were experiencing on the sea while Jesus was on shore. Include the time of day, condition of the sea, how far they were from shore, and what they were doing. (See also John 6:18–19 and Mark 6:48.)

The NIV translates the original Greek of Matthew 14:25 to be "shortly before dawn." However, it could be more literally translated as "during the fourth watch of the night." In ancient Rome, the nighttime hours from 6 p.m. to 6 a.m. were divided into four "watches" of three hours each. The fourth watch would be between 3 a.m. and 6 a.m.

10. Shortly before dawn, Jesus went out to meet the disciples by walking on the water. Understandably, this terrified them. It had already been a long night and now they saw a shadowy figure approaching them (Matthew 14:25–26). Imagine you are on the boat. What do you think you would be feeling or thinking, or what do you think you would say to the others when you saw someone walking on water toward you?

Mark 6:48 makes the additional note that Jesus was about to "pass by them." This makes it sound like Jesus was planning to just meet them on the other side of the lake. This is quite possible.

However, I think there is another interesting possibility. The use of these words "pass by" points to a passage in 1 Kings 19 where the prophet Elijah desperately needed encouragement from God. In this passage God told Elijah to go up the mountain because he (God) was "about to pass by" (1 Kings 19:11). As the Lord passed by, Elijah experienced God's presence as a gentle whisper. After this encounter Elijah received instruction and encouragement for how to move forward. It's possible that Mark is intentionally pointing to this Old Testament passage as evidence that Jesus is God and that following where he leads is best.

11. When the apostles caught sight of him, Jesus said, "Take courage! It is I. Don't be afraid." How do you think the disciples felt when they heard Jesus's voice and started to understand who it was?

12. Think about your life right now. What is an area of your life or a situation where you need courage? Close your eyes and imagine Jesus saying these words to you: "Take courage! Don't be afraid." What are some practical things you can do this week to help you take courage and not be afraid regarding this area or situation?

If you find yourself struggling with fear, read and/or memorize some of the following passages: Psalm 23; Matthew 6:25–34; and Philippians 4:6–8.

....

Set aside time to listen to and engage
with worship music today. Also, make
a plan for how you will be intentional
with your Sunday worship time.

Day 4
Stepping Out in Faith

Review Matthew 14:22–33.

13. Next to each verse from Matthew 14 listed below, write the
    words and/or actions of Jesus and Peter.

    Verse 28 (Peter):

    Verse 29 (Jesus):

    Verse 29 (Peter):

    Verse 30 (Peter):

    Verse 31 (Jesus):

14. Peter made a bold request of Jesus in verse 28. Why do you
    think Peter asked Jesus to tell him to come?

15. Jesus said "come" and Peter got out of the boat. What do you think Peter might have been thinking or feeling as he hung his feet over the edge of the boat? What do you think he might have been thinking or feeling as he let go of the side of the boat and stood on the water? What about when he took his first step away from the boat?

The boat was clearly the safest place to be while they were in the middle of the tumultuous waters. Getting out of the boat was risky and unsafe. I've always wondered why Peter wanted to get out of the boat in the first place. It doesn't seem very logical to me. Why didn't he just wait for Jesus to get into the boat?

However, as I've been reflecting on this passage, I think Peter wanted to be the kind of disciple who was truly covered in the dust of his rabbi, or in this case, the water. He didn't want to wait for Jesus to come to him; he wanted to go to Jesus. It's a bold picture of what discipleship looks like.

We all cling to things in our lives that give us a sense of safety and security. It could be your career or your home, your reputation or your bank account, even your relationships or your plans for the future. And yet Jesus wants us to be willing to let go of our ideal—to be willing to leave what may feel safe in order to follow where he is leading. He may not call you to leave behind something that brings security, but if he does, are you willing?

16. Flip back to question 13 in lesson 1 on page 28 where you reflected on a time when you felt like God asked you to do something that didn't make sense. How did that circumstance feel a little like getting out of your own boat of safety and security? What were some things that you had to leave behind that felt safe or secure? What happened imme-

diately after you got out of this "boat" and took your first steps of obedience? How did going through this experience impact your faith?

17. Is there something big or small you feel like you are being called to do that feels like a walking-on-water step of obedience? If you are hesitating, what's holding you back? Write a brief prayer asking God to help you be both discerning and brave. Consider sharing this with your group as your prayer request this week.

As part of your worship practice this week, take some time to listen to the worship song "You Make Me Brave" by Bethel Music (you can find a free version on YouTube). It's such a powerful and inspiring worship song. I love the reminder that it is Jesus who makes us brave. He is the one who calls us out beyond the shore into the waves.

....

Set aside time to listen to and engage with worship
music today. Also, make a plan for how you will
be intentional with your Sunday worship time.

Day 5
When Fear Comes

Review Matthew 14:22–33.

When Peter stepped out of the boat, he became one of only two
people who ever walked on water—the other being Jesus. Jesus,
while fully man, was also fully God, so it doesn't shock us to see
him defying these natural laws. But Peter was just a regular human
being, like you and me. When he took these first steps, he found
himself doing something that defied all logic and reason. Something
he had no ability to do on his own. He was walking on water.

But then he allowed fear to creep in. It's not hard to imagine why.
As a fisherman he knew that a powerful wind could capsize a boat
and drown even the most capable of swimmers. And now here he
was, fully exposed to the elements, no longer in the safety of a boat,
but standing on the water. He took his eyes off Jesus and turned his
focus toward the wind. Fear crested faster than the waves, and he
started sinking. In panic he cried out, "Lord, save me!"

18. Peter allowed his fear of the forceful wind to distract him
    from Jesus. Take a moment to brainstorm and list at least
    five things that make you afraid. How might these things
    distract you from keeping your eyes on Jesus?

    1.

    2.

    3.

4.

5.

19. Next to the fears you listed in question 18, write down how likely these things are to happen. If some of these fears are highly likely, realistically think through them and write down what it would be like for these fears to actually materialize.

Prayerfully pause to answer this next question as honestly as you can. If you are doing this study with a group, you will not be asked to share it. This is between you and the Lord.

20. Even if your fears materialize, do you think it's worth getting out of the "boat" to obediently follow Jesus? Why or why not?

21. What were the other disciples doing while Peter was walking on water (Matthew 14:33)? Do you think they wished they had gotten out of the boat too, or do you think they were glad they stayed in the boat?

22. Look back over this week's readings and capture the discipleship lessons you think Peter learned. The main discipleship lessons I think Peter learned were:

23. Flip back through week 2, including the practice section, and prayerfully ask the Lord to help you notice what he wants you to take away from this lesson. Ask yourself questions like: Did I learn something new? Do I feel like God is inviting me to trust or follow him in a new way? Is there a change I need to make? Or is there something else he seems to be drawing my attention to?

My takeaways are:

Peter took a huge risk and stepped out of the boat. It was just before dawn and darkness was still surrounding them. Getting out of the boat was not safe, nor was it sensible. But he wanted to follow and so he asked Jesus to call him. When Jesus did, Peter took a bold step of faithful obedience. While Peter was brave to step out in this way, he didn't do it perfectly. He was overcome by fear just moments later. When he felt the water thrash around him and spray into his face, he must have thought something like, *What was I thinking? I'm going to drown out here.* In that moment, he took his eyes off Jesus.

As I mentioned in lesson one, I was recently called to get out of one of my boats and leave my career of over twelve years in pastoral ministry at my local church. I've loved working and serving in this way—it has truly been the privilege of a lifetime. But God said it was time to move. Time for me get out of the boat. And in his kindness, he made it very clear to me. It hasn't been easy, though. More than once, fear has overwhelmed me with questions and doubts. In those moments, I get to choose to either focus on all the uncertainty or keep my eyes on Jesus. I'll be honest, I'm not doing it perfectly. I feel like I'm standing in the middle of a rocky sea right now. I've stepped away from the safety of what was known and I'm not quite on the solid ground of knowing where I'm headed. The good news is even when I let these fears take over, Jesus is always right beside me, always ready to extend his hand and steady me.

This is teaching me two things that I think Peter and the other disciples must have learned through this experience. First, Jesus never left Peter. He was there the whole time. Peter took his eyes off Jesus, but Jesus never took his eyes off Peter.

Second, the eleven who stayed in the boat were not stripped of their titles as disciples, but they didn't get to have the same experience that Peter had. By staying in the boat, they lost out on walking on water. They only got to hear what it was like. They didn't get to experience the thrill or the fear, but Jesus still called them his disciples and still invited them to take steps of bold faith moving forward.

If you feel like God is inviting you to take a bold step of faith, know that I'm praying for you to have courage to do it. I can almost guarantee you that it won't be easy. But I know Jesus is there and he will not take his eyes off you.

PRACTICE REFLECTION

1. As you intentionally engaged in communal worship at your church this week, did you notice anything different from other times you attend church?

2. As you chose to worship each day through intentionally engaging with worship music, did you notice any changes in how you thought or felt about God or a situation you are facing? If so, describe what happened.

3. Was there a song that was particularly meaningful to you? If so, what was it and why? If you are doing this study with a group, make a list of the songs your group shares and spend some time listening to them this coming week.

CONFESSIONS AND COSTS

Day 1
Practice: Sharing Jesus with Others

I heard something interesting about one of my friends. Apparently, he asks almost every waitress or waiter how he can pray for them. I wondered how this question came across. Did they think he was weird? Did they spit in his food? Did they just look at him confused and walk away? To be honest, I felt like it was a little more than a bold move; I thought it was kind of weird.

And then I witnessed it. We were with a group and at the end of the meal he looked at our waitress and asked, "Hey, how can I pray for you?"

She stopped dead in her tracks and looked him in the eye. She got a little teary as she said, "I'm a single mom and I'm working this job and I'm also in school trying to make a better life for my daughter. It's really hard, though. I'm exhausted and tempted to give up. Can you pray that I'll keep going and find the strength to get through this?"

Umm. Wow. That was not at all what I was expecting.

He leaned in and asked her a few more questions. What was she studying? How old was her daughter? He said he would definitely pray and then pointed to the rest of us and said, "We all will."

She was no longer some random woman who brought my food and refreshed my water. She was a person with a story. She had hopes and dreams. She was discouraged. She was working hard to make a life for herself.

And let me tell you, I most definitely prayed for her. Many times.

When we were leaving, she thanked us again for being so kind. And we did leave her a nice tip—because words without meaningful action would have defeated the purpose. She caught a glimpse of Jesus that day through my friend. He didn't share the whole gospel with her, but he did plant a seed. And seed planting matters. God tells us our job is to simply plant the seeds; he will take care of making them grow (1 Corinthians 3:6–7).

We can plant seeds so many ways. It can be a simple question like, "How can I pray for you?" Or maybe it is telling a neighbor or friend how you got through a hard season because of your faith. Or it could even be doing something kind for someone and then following it up with words that tell them your kindness is because of Jesus. This week, I want to encourage you to be intentional and plant a few seeds. To do this, start with prayer and ask God if there is someone specific he wants you to share with. If a name comes to mind, write it in the margin. Then pray about how you can use your words and actions to share Jesus with that person. Also ask him to help you see and be willing to boldly seize spur-of-the-moment opportunities.

In our lesson this week, Peter made a bold confession about who Jesus is. Knowing who Jesus really is changes everything. It changes our now and our forever. He is news worth sharing. I pray this practice of sharing Jesus will be life-giving for you and others.

Intentionally plant seeds by telling
others about Jesus this week.

Day 2
Who Do People Say I Am?

Read Matthew 16:13–20.

The disciples continued following and learning from Jesus. At this point in the journey, Jesus wanted to make sure they were beginning to understand who he was and what he had come to do. While Peter did seem to have some comprehension of this, he still had a long way to go.

The first thing he needed to learn was that Jesus had come this time to be a suffering servant, not a conquering king. You see, during Peter's time, God-fearing Jews suffered under the tyranny of Roman occupation and longed for the freedom and restoration of their nation. They believed God would do this for them, but they had a shortsighted vision of how it would happen. They thought he would send a powerful earthly king to defeat Rome and elevate Israel. What they failed to understand was that God's plan for restoration was much bigger than geography or national affiliation. It would be redemption for all time and all people— Jews and non-Jews alike.

To do this, God sent Jesus as the one who was able to pay the penalty for sin and redeem all of humanity through his death and resurrection. Although this truth can be seen throughout the entire Old Testament, it remained clouded for most of Jesus's contemporaries. So, when Jesus started clarifying what was coming next, it confused Peter and the other disciples.

﹅

A quick clarification on the first and second comings of Jesus. Jesus's first coming was to bring salvation to humanity through his sinless life, death on the cross, and resurrection. All that is required is our faith. At his second coming, he will return and reign as the true King that he is. The Jews misunderstood this and thought he would only come as a conquering king.

....

Peter pushed back and I honestly can't blame him. I love Jesus; he is my Lord and my Savior. But he was even more to Peter—he was also his very real friend, probably his best friend. I've often wondered what I would have said to Jesus if I had been there. I'm certain I would have tried to find alternatives to the kind of death and suffering Jesus described.

And that leads us to the second thing Peter needed to learn—discipleship is costly. Jesus wasn't the only one called to make a significant sacrifice; Peter and the others were called to do the same. And so are we. While journeying with Jesus should bring much joy and fulfillment, it will also bring opportunities for great sacrifice. But even in those moments that feel sacrificial, it will always be worth it.

1. Jesus asked the disciples, "Who do people say the Son of Man is?" They responded with a lengthy list of what people were saying. (See also John 10:19–20.) Thinking about the world we live in, what are some things people say today about who Jesus is?

2. Why do you think most people didn't know who Jesus was? There are probably many reasons, but look up Matthew 11:27 for one of the main ones. Why do you think people don't know who Jesus is today?

3. Jesus then asked the disciples more pointedly, "But what about you? Who do you say I am?" The "you" in this question is plural, meaning Jesus was asking the entire group of twelve. Based on what we've been learning about Peter, why do you think he answered the question instead of another disciple? How do you think he felt about speaking up in this way?

4. This wasn't the first time a declaration was made about the identity of Jesus. Look up the following passages where Jesus is identified partially or fully. (They are listed in roughly chronological order.) What was similar and different about these confessions? You'll want to examine what was said, who was saying it, and what had just happened.

John 1:41

John 1:49

Matthew 14:33

Mark 1:23–24

Based on these verses and Jesus's response to Peter, do you think Peter's confession was different than the others? If so, why?

Messiah simply means "anointed one." Throughout the Old Testament it was a term that was given to someone who had been set apart and empowered by God for special work, like the kings and priests of Israel. However, later in the Old Testament, the term *Messiah* started to take on a narrower and more sacred meaning (for example, in Daniel 9:25–26). The Israelites still didn't know exactly what it meant, but they knew they were waiting on the one who would be set apart in an even more special way than priests or kings were.

5. If Jesus asked you, "But what about you? Who do you say I am?" what would you say? Feel free to answer with more words than Peter did. Consider things like who he is, what he has done, his character, etc.

When I think about this question, I realize how much the answer has changed over the years—and keeps changing. In the beginning I knew he was God's Son sent to save me, and so I would answer this question accurately by stating he is my Savior. Today this answer is still very true. However, my relationship with Jesus has grown and changed. Now I would add that he is also my friend, my God, the one I follow, the lover of my soul, the one who accepts me no matter what. The list goes on and on. I have not plumbed the depths of who Jesus is, and that makes my relationship with him even more real. Just like in any relationship, we will continue to discover more about Jesus as we spend more time with him.

Intentionally plant seeds by telling
others about Jesus this week.

Day 3
A New Identity

Review Matthew 16:13–20.

Peter made an accurate statement that Jesus's true identity was
the Messiah and the Son of God. It's important to note that God
was the one who revealed this information to Peter. It wasn't
because Peter was observant, had discovered something new, or
just figured it out. It was inspired knowledge graciously given to
him from God. It's also important to realize that while Peter was
able to give this accurate confession of who Jesus was, he still
didn't fully understand all that it meant.

6. Do you recall the first time you were able to make a similar
    profession about the deity of Jesus? If so, what led up to
    your doing this? How do you think God was involved in
    this situation? If you have always known who Jesus is, to
    answer the previous questions think of a time when your
    understanding of him changed significantly. If you haven't
    ever made this kind of declaration about the deity of Jesus,
    what do you think is holding you back? Ask God to enable
    you to understand who Jesus is and then talk and pray with
    a trusted Christian leader or friend about your questions.

7. Thinking back to when you first heard about Jesus, how has your understanding of who he is changed as you've gotten to know him more? If you are doing this as a group, make sure to share as a way to encourage each other about who he is and what he means to you.

8. After Peter stated who Jesus is, Jesus called Peter blessed and emphasized Peter's new name and what Peter would do. Read again Jesus's first words to Peter in John 1:42. Why do you think it's significant that Jesus reminded Peter of his new name? What additional information did Jesus add? Why do you think this is significant?

9. When we become followers of Jesus by faith, we are also given a new identity. Match the following verses with who you are now that you know Jesus.

I am chosen.	Psalm 139:13–14
I am wonderfully made, created on purpose.	John 1:12
I am his handiwork and masterpiece.	John 15:15
I am holy and righteous.	John 15:16
I am his friend.	Ephesians 2:10
I am his child.	Ephesians 4:24

10. You probably won't get to hear an audible response like Jesus gave to Peter in Matthew 16:17, but imagine what Jesus might speak over you today about your new identity. Fill in the blanks below using your name and what you think he might say. (Keep in mind, as long as what you say doesn't contradict Scripture, then there are no wrong answers.) For example, I might fill it out as follows:

※

"The Enemy will try to convince you that you're not enough, but through the power of God's Word, you can send that viper back where he belongs. If Christ sits on the throne of your life, then he retains the final say about who you are, what you're called to do, and what you're capable of."[1]

—Margaret Feinberg

Blessed are you, Jodie, for this was not revealed to you by flesh and blood, but by my Father in heaven. And now I tell you, my beloved daughter, leave your old ways behind, learn about me, and follow wherever I lead. I want you to help others become my disciples too.

Blessed are you, _____, for this was not revealed to you by flesh and blood, but by my Father in heaven. And now I tell you _____

_____

_____

_____

_____

_____

_____

_____

This passage concludes with Jesus giving the disciples strict orders not to tell anyone who he is. This seems counterintuitive to us—after all, wouldn't it be better to spread the news? But Jesus knew the people weren't quite ready to know who he truly is. They were waiting on a savior, but their view of what this person would do was shortsighted. They wanted someone to solve their immediate problems. Yet Jesus was here to do so much more. He was here to bring salvation to the entire world throughout all time. He knew that if people found out his identity too soon, they would try to stand in the way of his ultimate purpose and make him their king by force (John 6:15).

Intentionally plant seeds by telling
others about Jesus this week.

Day 4
Never, Lord!

Read Matthew 16:21–23.

Peter's confession on behalf of the disciples marked a significant
turning point for Jesus. From that point forward he was more
forthright that he would suffer, die, and be raised back to life.
Matthew 16:21 indicates that Jesus was very clear about what
was coming and yet, as we will see in coming lessons, the disciples still didn't get it.

11. Peter and Jesus had a strong interaction over the fact that
    Jesus would suffer and die. In your own words, write what
    they said to one another. Imagine you are Peter. Why do
    you think he had such a strong reaction to what Jesus was
    telling them?

12. Have you ever had a close friend or relative start down a road that you knew would be hard for them (for either good or bad)? How did you react? How does this help you identify with Peter's reaction?

13. What name does Jesus call Peter in verse 23? Compare this with how he identified him in verse 18 and what he told Peter he would do. Why do you think Jesus made this pivot in how he identified Peter?

14. Just like Peter wasn't really a "rock," he also wasn't really "Satan." However, Jesus's statement indicates that he was no longer acting like a rock but was acting on behalf of Satan. Write a brief summary next to each of the following verses for why Jesus needed to die. Considering the truth in these verses, how had Peter become a stumbling block to Jesus by acting on behalf of Satan?

Romans 3:23

Romans 6:23

2 Corinthians 5:21

15. Jesus told Peter that he didn't have in mind the concerns of God, but merely human concerns. What do you think were Peter's human concerns? How could he have responded if he was considering the concerns of God?

16. Consider your life. What are some of the human concerns on your heart right now (for example: fear of the future, relationship distress, children, finances, pain, loneliness, etc.)? How can you turn these concerns over to the Lord and entrust them to him?

The concerns you listed above are real, and many of them won't simply vanish after you turn them over to the Lord. However, you can still seek to have the concerns of God at the front of your mind instead of your earthly concerns. That doesn't mean if you need a job, you should avoid looking for one. Nor does it mean you shouldn't work on your relationship if it feels broken or seek out community if you are lonely. It simply means you do it with a different perspective—trusting that God is good, that he hasn't taken his eyes off of you, and that ultimately he is working things out for your best.

I know firsthand how hard it can be when doubt, fear, and confusion take over. It is a mental battle to turn these things over to God and reclaim the truth. Jesus is a great example for us in doing this. Of course, he didn't *want* to go through suffering and die at the hands of his enemies. Who would? However, this was actually the very best thing for him to do and so he stayed the course and trusted God each step of the way. It didn't make sense to Peter in that moment that Jesus's death was part of God's plan, just like our trials often don't make sense to us. But if we can reclaim the truth of who God is and what he has done for us, even if we have to do it a thousand times a day, we can begin to move toward having his concerns be top priorities in our mind versus being overrun by our own.

Intentionally plant seeds by telling
others about Jesus this week.

Day 5
The Cost of Discipleship

Review Matthew 16:23–28.

I've often wondered what Peter thought of this interaction with
Jesus. He went from the high praise of being called blessed to
being called Satan in what reads like it was a matter of minutes.
Of course, it could have been days between these two interactions, but Matthew wants us to see the juxtaposition of Peter
being an ally one minute and an adversary the next. I'm pretty
sure Peter didn't know he was stepping in the way of Jesus's
plans; I think he was just trying to be a good friend. After all, no
one wants to see their friend suffer.

But being comfortable and avoiding suffering was never God's
goal. It wasn't for Jesus, it couldn't be for the disciples, and it
can't be for us either. Although Peter was the one who spoke up,
all the disciples must have been thinking the same thing because
Jesus turned to address them all.

This is a hard passage to read and digest because while it was
spoken to the disciples, it is also written for us. Journeying with
Jesus isn't all sunshine and roses. It costs us something, as anything of value should.

17. Place a circle around the three things Jesus said the twelve needed to do if they wanted to be his disciples.

"Then Jesus said to his disciples, 'Whoever wants to be my disciple must deny themselves and take up their cross and follow me.'" (Matthew 16:24)

In Peter's day, the cross was a cruel way to impose death on someone who was guilty of a serious crime, similar to how we might view a hanging today. When Jesus used this symbolic language, it was understood that he was calling them to a total and complete commitment to him, no matter the costs, even unto death.

18. The first thing Jesus stated was that the disciples needed to deny themselves. Based on what we have studied so far, how do you think the disciples, and especially Peter, needed to deny themselves? Is there an area where you feel like you need to "deny yourself" so you can follow Jesus? Brainstorm some practical ways you could do this.

19. The second thing Jesus told the disciples they needed to do was "take up their cross." What are some of the ways the disciples needed to "take up their cross"? Is there a "cross" you need to pick up so you can follow Jesus? What are some practical steps you can take to start doing this?

20. According to Matthew 16:25–27, what are some of the benefits of doing these things? How does considering this help you with some of the areas you identified in the previous questions?

In this passage, Jesus stated that he will return and reward each person for what they have done. This can get confusing because there are actually two judgments Scripture teaches us about. The one Jesus refers to in this passage is the second judgment and is called the Judgment Seat of Christ, or the Bema Seat. It is a judgment only for believers. During this judgment, our works will be shown for what they truly were. The things that were worthless burn away and what is left will be rewarded by Jesus (1 Corinthians 3:12–15). There is no punishment at this judgment, only reward.

The other judgment happens first and is often called the Great White Throne Judgment. At this judgment, every single person stands before God and only those who have faith in Jesus are invited to enter into eternal life with him (Revelation 20:11–15). If you are a follower of Jesus, you do not need to fear either judgment. However, this first judgment should motivate us to share Jesus with others, so that they are invited into eternal life with God. And the Bema Seat judgment should motivate us to follow wherever God leads us, because we will be rewarded for these good works.

21. Look back over this week's readings and note the discipleship lessons you think Peter learned. The main discipleship lessons I think Peter learned were:

22. Flip back through week 3, including the practice section, and prayerfully ask the Lord to help you notice what he wants you to take away from this lesson. Ask yourself questions like: Did I learn something new? Do I feel like God is inviting me to trust or follow him in a new way? Is there a change I need to make? Or is there something else he seems to be drawing my attention to?

My takeaways are:

I know some of these questions, especially over the last two days, were really difficult to consider, but I hope you prayerfully leaned in and asked God what he wanted you to see. I could have simply asked you one question, "What really holds you back from fully following Jesus?"

The truth is many things hold us back. It is incredibly easy to get consumed by our fears and concerns. The Enemy would like nothing more than to distract and derail you with these things. But Jesus is calling you to trust him and live in a better way. It does require that we lay aside whatever holds us back, but thankfully, he's not asking for all sacrifice with no reward. As you read, there is reward coming, but there are also real benefits now. For example, Jesus tells us that he came to give us a full and abundant life (John 10:10) and that following him brings peace (Philippians 4:9). Those two things alone are worth fully following him. I want my life to be marked by his peace and abundance. Don't you?

Keep up the good work, my friend. We are on an amazing journey of discovering what it looks like to follow Jesus. He is worth it. And I think Peter would be the first in line to tell you that.

PRACTICE REFLECTION

1. Were you able to "plant a seed" by sharing Jesus in some way this week? If so, what did you do and what happened?

2. Did you learn anything new about yourself or God through this activity? If so, what?

ARE YOU LISTENING?

Day 1
Practice: Listening Well to Love Well

I have a friend who is a great listener. I actually have a few of them, but the one I'm thinking of is particularly good at being fully engaged whenever we are together. She leans in as she listens, she doesn't interrupt, and she always asks great questions. Whenever we spend time together, I leave feeling full. Feeling loved. Feeling known. Everyone needs a friend like her. (But I'm not telling you who she is, because I'm a little selfish that way.) Being her friend has challenged me to be a better listener for others (especially her).

Listening is a skill. A skill that, if we are honest, we aren't inherently good at. I've found that when I'm listening to someone, I naturally do a few things. First, I think about what I want to say when they're done talking. Second, I think about what I want to say when they're done talking. OK fine, the only thing I do is think about what I want to say. Now before you decide never to have a conversation with me, notice I said it's what I naturally do. I've been working on my listening skills for years. And while I don't always get it right, I do think I've grown quite a bit. Now when someone tells me they need to talk, I intentionally pause and say a quick prayer asking the Lord to help me listen well and to notice what he wants me to see. I also do my best to not offer unsolicited advice or quick fixes, but to simply ask them questions. When I do this, I find that the person who wanted to talk feels loved and seen by me.

I've learned that listening and asking good questions is a profound way to show love. Especially in our world today. To prove my point, let's do a little experiment. First, think about the last time someone asked you a meaningful question and then really listened to you. Write in the margin who that was and how it made you feel. For me, it was just the other night sitting around a table with some young women. One of them looked over at me and said, "Tell me who you are. I'd love to know who Jodie is." I was a bit caught off guard, but I believed she really wanted to know so I told her. It kicked off a great conversation.

Now, on the flip side, think of times when you needed to talk to someone and they either cut you off, started telling you about when something like that happened to them, or were distracted by their phone or watch. You don't need to write their names down, but do write in the margin how it made you feel. I'm guessing that moment was frustrating and quite possibly hurtful. I know when it happens to me, I feel overlooked, and I shut down pretty quickly. I don't want to share my heart with someone who doesn't really want to hear it.

This week we will study a passage where Peter learns the importance of listening well—specifically to Jesus. One of the ways Jesus summarized his teaching was by telling us to love God and love others as we love ourselves (Matthew 22:37–39). I want to make the case, which I think is easy to make, that one essential way we can love well is to listen well. Listening to God and listening to others. This week we are going to intentionally practice both of these.

To start your practice, first pray and ask God to help you be ready to listen when the opportunity arises. Then ask him to help you recognize whom he wants you to listen to. If a name comes to mind, jot it below. Next consider how you could spend some intentional time with that person this week. It might be asking someone to coffee, taking a walk after dinner, or even just intentionally stopping by a coworker's desk. Keep in mind that it doesn't have to be a super long conversation—it just needs to be a time to start listening. Finally, when you are with the person, ask questions and then listen. Now, of course you need to be responsive and engaged in the conversation; don't sit there like a stone wall, but the point is to let the other person do most of the talking. Nod, be engaged, and say things like, "Tell me more about that." See what happens.

Later in the week I'll guide you into an activity to help you create space to listen to God. For now, put on your listening ears for others.

What is your plan for whom you will listen to and how you will make space to do this?

PRACTICE REMINDER

Create space to intentionally listen to
someone, or multiple people, this week.

Day 2
Drawing Away

Read Luke 9:28–36.

This passage comes directly after the one we studied in the last lesson, which, as a reminder, was where Jesus started to tell the disciples he would suffer at the hands of the religious leaders of the day. At this point in the journey, Jesus's reputation was preceding him. People were seeking him out everywhere he went. They were challenged by his teaching and captivated by his miracles. The religious leaders, however, had a much different reaction to him. In their eyes, he was disrupting their well-established systems and was a problem that needed to be eradicated as quickly as possible. Thus, they were looking for any reason they could to arrest and charge Jesus, and he knew it.

Jesus knew this would happen but that didn't mean he was immune to feeling discouraged by it. Don't forget that Jesus, while fully God, was also fully human. This means he experienced the full range of emotions. It would be critical for him to stay close to God the Father so he could be strengthened and encouraged by him, especially during his last days and weeks.

The story you read today is often referred to as "The Transfiguration." It's told three times in the Gospels: Matthew 17:1–13; Mark 9:2–13; and Luke 9:28–36. Each writer shares different details about the encounter. We will focus on the accounts of Matthew and Luke, but if you have time, read the passage in Mark. I've asked you to read the whole story in Luke today so you can understand the context of the story, but we are only focusing on the first few verses for now.

1. Why did Jesus take the three apostles and go up on the mountain? (See Luke 9:28–29. Also consider Mark 1:35 and Matthew 14:23.) Why do you think Jesus needed this time with God?

You may wonder why Jesus only took Peter, James, and John on this excursion. Scripture doesn't tell us explicitly, but we do know they were the first disciples who left everything to follow him (Luke 5:8–11). We also know this isn't the only time he singled them out. In Mark 5:35–43 they witnessed Jesus raising the recently deceased twelve-year-old daughter of Jairus, a synagogue ruler. And then in Mark 14:32–42, Jesus took them into the garden of Gethsemane, just before he was arrested, and asked them to watch and pray while he went off alone to pray.

These passages lead us to believe that Peter, James, and John were his closest companions. All twelve disciples were called to follow, but these men were invited into places the others were not. We can be assured Jesus wasn't playing favorites; rather, he was preparing these three for carrying additional responsibilities when he was gone.

2. Knowing that Jesus wasted nothing, and all of his time and words were being used to prepare Peter and the others for when he would leave, what do you think Jesus was trying to teach Peter about how to be in relationship with God?

The lessons Jesus was trying to teach Peter were reinforced through other interactions. Let's look at one account that happened after the transfiguration and holds similar instruction.

3. Read Luke 10:38–42. This is an account that Peter would have witnessed. Next to each name, summarize what each woman did and how she responded to Jesus.

Mary:

Martha:

Why do you think Jesus said Mary had chosen what was better? What do you think this means about getting needed work done?

4. What do you think Peter learned from watching this interaction between Mary, Martha, and Jesus? How do you think this reinforced the lessons he learned at the transfiguration and throughout his journey with Jesus?

"One of the surest signs that [Martha's] life is out of order is the fact that she even tells Jesus what to do: 'Tell her to help me!' Mary, on the other hand, is active in a different way. She sits at the feet of Jesus, listening to him. She . . . prioritizes *being with* Jesus over *doing for* Jesus."[1]

—Peter Scazzero

Jesus made this point again and again. If he needed time alone with God, how much more did Peter? How much more do we? Jesus knew the demands of ministry would be incredibly difficult for Peter. Peter would probably be tempted to just keep going and working for God without taking time to draw away and be alone with him. This is an incredible temptation for us too. Our lives are jam-packed with things to do—work, errands, family, friends, serving and loving others—the list is endless. Truly, there is no shortage of things and people that need our attention. It's very easy to get pulled into *doing for* God at the expense of *being with* him. I'm a lot like Martha. When I see all the work that needs to be done, I have a hard time sitting still at Jesus's feet.

Notice, though, that Jesus didn't say the work was bad; he simply said that Mary had chosen what was better. She was choosing being with over doing for. The doing would have still happened. The table may not have been as perfect nor the food as delightful, but no one would have gone hungry—and more importantly their souls would be fuller than their bellies.

This is a critical discipleship lesson that Peter needed, and so do we. We cannot fully follow Jesus if we aren't taking time to be with him.

5. In your own life, how do you make time to be with Jesus? What are some of the things that threaten to distract you and tend to pull you away from this time? What adjustments do you need to make?

What are some practical ways you can make these adjustments? (For example, if you know you need to spend more consistent time in God's Word, instead of just telling yourself to do it, brainstorm how you could do this. You might come up with ideas like: I will get up ten minutes earlier; I

will commit to not looking at my phone until I have read
God's Word, etc.)

Know that if you just identified a place where you need to make
an adjustment, there is no shame. We all get distracted and get
sucked into *doing* mode. I want to encourage you to simply recognize it and then hit the reset button. God is always ready for
us to *be* with him.

PRACTICE REMINDER

Create space to intentionally listen to
someone, or multiple people, this week.

Day 3
Transformed

Read Matthew 17:1–13.

Like yesterday, I'm asking you to read the whole story of the
transfiguration, but this time in Matthew, so you can see the
verses we are studying in context of the whole story.

"Transfiguration" in Matthew 17:2 comes from the Greek
word *metamorphoo*. This is the same word we use for metamor-
phosis, which, you may remember from middle school, is what
a caterpillar does when it becomes a butterfly. *Metamorphoo*
means to be fully transformed or completely changed.

6. What happened to Jesus's appearance? (See also Luke
   9:29.) What do you think Jesus's change in appearance
   could mean about his encounter with God?

7. We will look at Peter's missteps during this encounter to-
   morrow, but for now, imagine what this might have been
   like for Peter, James, and John. What do you think they
   were thinking and feeling as they saw the transfiguration?

8. This experience made a lasting impact on Peter. Read 2 Peter 1:16–18, which is where Peter wrote about this experience years later. Why do you think he starts with defending that the account was not a "cleverly devised story"? What do you think it meant that Jesus received "honor and glory from God"? How do you think this encounter, including the words spoken over Jesus, might have helped Jesus prepare for what was coming?

9. Peter also summarized this encounter by stating they were "eyewitnesses of his majesty." What do you think this means? How do you think witnessing the transfiguration of Jesus impacted Peter and his ability to follow Jesus?

10. Look up the word *majesty* in a dictionary. List some ways that you have witnessed God's majesty recently (for example, the sun rising each morning or a specific answered prayer). How does this list encourage you as you seek to be a faithful follower of Jesus?

Jesus was transformed, made completely different, right before Peter's eyes. When we become believers in Jesus, we are also transformed. Second Corinthians 5:17 tells us that we become a new creation through our faith in Jesus. What an amazing truth. And while it is one hundred percent true spiritually, our experience tells us that physically we aren't completely new just yet. We still live in our aging bodies, in a sinful and broken world, and this means that we will still wrestle

"Therefore, if anyone is in Christ, the new creation has come: The old has gone, the new is here!"
—2 Corinthians 5:17

with our own sin until Jesus returns. However, because of Jesus we can and should experience victory over many of our sins as we turn them over to Jesus and choose what he wants for us (Romans 6:6–7).

11. Read 2 Corinthians 5:17 in the margin. In what ways are you new and/or different because of your faith in Jesus? In what ways do you still wrestle with things that feel like they qualify as your old sinful nature?

12. Read Romans 12:2. The same word, *metamorphoo*, that is used in Matthew 17:2 is used here. How does this verse say we can experience transformation? What are some ways you can do this with the area(s) you identified in the previous question? What would be the benefits of this transformation?

Create space to intentionally listen to
someone, or multiple people, this week.

Day 4
Divine Interruptions

Read Matthew 17:5–8.

The text tells us that while the transfiguration was occuring, Jesus had a conversation with Moses and Elijah, two men from the Old Testament who were long deceased. In Scripture Moses represents the Old Testament Law, which is the first five books of the Bible, and Elijah represents the Prophets, which symbolized the rest of the Old Testament. Thus, Jesus was talking with two people who represented the fullness of what had come before him. And the Old Testament text, along with these men, prophesied and pointed to Jesus's coming all along (Luke 24:27).

13. What happened while Peter was speaking? Notice that this means Peter was interrupted. Why do you think God cut him off mid-thought?

14. Compare Matthew 17:5 with Matthew 3:18, which is what God spoke over Jesus directly after his baptism. What is similar and what is different? Why do you think God made this statement twice about Jesus?

15. This was probably the first time Peter heard God's audible voice—and it was partly to command him to listen to Jesus. How did Peter react? What do you think this part of the experience was like for Peter?

Peter fell facedown and was terrified. I think given the circumstances, that seems reasonable. He'd seen a glowing Jesus, observed two dead men, and heard God's audible voice. I can't imagine I would respond much differently. When Jesus touched Peter and told him to get up and not be afraid, I think he had compassion in his voice. He knew this experience was a lot to process for a mere mortal.

16. Read James 1:22. According to this verse and what you know about listening to God, what do you think God meant when he told Peter to listen?

17. Spend a moment reflecting on your relationship with God. Do you feel like you ever hear from God? If so, how does he speak to you? Are there things you have done to help you learn to hear his voice? If you don't hear from God, why do you think this is?

Create space to intentionally listen to
someone, or multiple people, this week.

Day 5
Cultivating a Listening Heart

Read Mark 9:7–12.

18. There are many ways we can cultivate attentiveness to bet-
    ter hear God's voice. Read the following Scriptures and
    write what they reveal about some ways we can hear from
    God.

    "For the word of God is alive and powerful. It is sharper
    than the sharpest two-edged sword, cutting between
    soul and spirit, between joint and marrow. It exposes our
    innermost thoughts and desires." (Hebrews 4:12 NLT)

    "Be still, and know that I am God." (Psalm 46:10)

    "All Scripture is God-breathed and is useful for teach-
    ing, rebuking, correcting and training in righteous-
    ness." (2 Timothy 3:16)

    "While they were worshiping the Lord and fasting, the
    Holy Spirit said, 'Set apart for me Barnabas and Saul
    for the work to which I have called them.' So after more
    fasting and prayer, the men laid their hands on them
    and sent them on their way." (Acts 13:2)

"Call to me and I will answer you and tell you great and unsearchable things you do not know." (Jeremiah 33:3)

"Take delight in the LORD, and he will give you the desires of your heart." (Psalm 37:4)

God cut Peter off and spoke over him so he could say what really needed to be said. While God can absolutely cut us off mid-sentence and speak to us in this way, today he speaks more in the quiet moments when we are being attentive to his voice and seeking to listen to him. (See 1 Kings 19:11–13 for a great example of this.) One of the ways we can seek to be attentive is through a practice of intentional and prayerful silence.

As you may recall from our practice section in day one, in addition to creating space to listen to others, I stated that we would create some space to listen to God. This practice will take you about five minutes. I'll guide you each step of the way.

Before we get started there are two things I want to tell you. First, you will need to find a place where you can be undistracted for at least five minutes. Second, our goal is to enter into silence with the desire to just be present with God and to not fill the space with our own words and agenda. He may have something to say to you; if he does, listen and, at the end, write down what you feel you've heard. But if God seems silent, then just enjoy the space of being with him.

19. First, find a comfortable and quiet place where you can be undisturbed for a few minutes. Grab your phone or a timer and set it for four or five minutes. If you've never done this before, four minutes may feel long. If you do a practice like this regularly, you may want to set the timer longer.

    Next, choose a short verse or phrase to recite slowly whenever your mind wanders. Try one of these or another verse that comes to mind.

"Be still, and know that I am God." (Psalm 46:10)

"The LORD is my shepherd." (Psalm 23:1)

"Not my will, but yours." (Luke 22:42)

"You are my refuge." (Psalm 46:1)

Take a few deep breaths to settle your mind and heart and then start the timer. Enjoy this peaceful place with the Lord.

Take a few minutes to write about the experience using the following questions or anything else that comes to mind. What did you enjoy? Was there anything that made you uncomfortable? Did God seem near, far, or something else? Did you hear anything you think could have been from the Lord? If so, what was it?

"[Silence] enables us to withdraw not only from the noise and distraction of the external world, but also the 'noise' of the inner compulsions that drive us. In solitude and silence, we become quiet enough to hear a voice that is not our own. This is the Voice we most need to hear."[2]
—Ruth Haley Barton

20. As they were walking down the mountain, what did Jesus tell Peter, James, and John in Matthew 17:9? Why do you think this was important? What detail does Mark 9:9–10 add? Do you think they understood yet? Why or why not?

The rest of the conversation down the mountain centered around Elijah and their trying to reconcile what they had just seen with what they had been taught. They had been taught to expect Elijah to come as the one who would prepare the way for the Lord (Malachi 4:5–6). Jesus pointed them to John the Baptist who, spiritually speaking, fulfilled the role of Elijah by preparing the way for Jesus (Matthew 3:1–3; 11:10–15).

In the end, while Peter didn't fully understand everything that happened on the mountain, he did begin to understand that the Old Testament prophecies were being fulfilled right before his eyes. Jesus was the one he, and the world, had been waiting for.

21. Look back over this week's readings and capture the discipleship lessons you think Peter learned. The main discipleship lessons I think Peter learned were:

22. Flip back through week 4, including the practice section, and prayerfully ask the Lord to help you notice what he wants you to take away from this lesson. Ask yourself questions like: Did I learn something new? Do I feel like God is inviting me to trust or follow him in a new way? Is there a change I need to make? Or is there something else he seems to be drawing my attention to?

    My takeaways are:

I hope you will create space to continue practicing being still and silent with the Lord. It truly is a discipline for me to do this practice, but when I do it, I find that it brings me deep peace. Just this morning I sat in silence and stillness with the Lord. Everything about me felt jumpy, especially my mind. And so, I kept going back to Psalm 23:1, "The LORD is my shepherd, I lack nothing." I didn't hear anything specific from the Lord, but my heart settled and my body relaxed. When I was done with my time of silence, I had a renewed awareness that God had everything well under control. There's something about this posture of surrender, of sitting with God without any agenda, that helps me remember that he is in control, and I am not. I hope you will discover this too.

PRACTICE REFLECTION

1. Did God bring someone to mind for you to have a listening conversation with this week? If so, were you able to set aside some time to intentionally listen to this person? What happened?

2. Did you learn anything new about yourself or God through this activity?

HUMBLE SERVANT

Day 1
Practice: Serving Others

A few years ago, my father passed away unexpectedly. Nothing will ever prepare you for a call like that. He was sick, but he was getting better. It just didn't seem right. Death never does.

It wasn't long before news spread and there was a knock on my door. My friend hugged me and said, "I just wanted to check on you. You don't need to say anything, I just wanted to let you know I'm here and I love you." We sat for a few moments in teary silence. Then the next morning another friend came and dropped off some little Bundt cakes. Shortly after that another friend showed up with a meal. And it just kept happening—treats arrived, lunches were delivered, and my mailbox swelled with condolences. Friends at work went above and beyond to take things off my plate so I could be available to take care of my family and myself. I was surrounded and supported in a way I've never really experienced before.

Most people didn't even ask me what I needed, they just showed up and offered something. If they had asked, I would have told them I wasn't sure what I needed. I would have told them I was

OK on food. I would have told them I could figure it out. And truly, I could have. But thankfully I didn't have to.

Their sacrificial acts of love and care were tangible reminders that God saw me and cared for me. Even though I was going through something very difficult, I knew I was not alone. I've always known that serving others was important, but through this experience I came to know, in a very personal way, how service lightens the load and lifts the spirit. And while I would never wish these circumstances on anyone, I do wish everyone could have a similar experience of being loved and cared for in this way.

As I'm sure you've already guessed, this week our practice is to serve someone as a way to show them the love and care of Jesus. Service, as we will see in this lesson, is something Jesus practiced and taught his disciples to do as well—even when it was messy and inconvenient.

Start by asking the Lord if there is someone in particular he wants you to serve this week. If a name comes to mind, jot it down in the margin. Then brainstorm what you could do that would be helpful to this person. Some ideas could be taking them a meal (even a store-bought one), providing a few hours of care for their kids, or writing out a thoughtful prayer and sending it in the mail. Although it will be tempting to ask your friends what they need, chances are they won't really know. So, if you do feel compelled to ask, give them a this or that option. For example, you could say something like, "I'd love to help you this week. Can I bring you dinner or mow your lawn?"

If you don't feel like the Lord gives you a name, then ask him each morning to help you be ready to serve whenever the opportunity arises. It could be helping someone pay for groceries, taking lunch to your coworker who got slammed with an unexpected meeting, or caring for your neighbor's kids last minute. It's hard to say what opportunities will arise, but I believe that if you are prayerfully open, God will give you an opportunity to serve someone. Even what may feel like a small opportunity can be an incredible expression of love to someone.

No matter what you do, be prepared for two things. First, you will be inconvenienced. Serving someone almost always requires sacrifice of time, money, or another resource. But second, when you do it out of a heart of love for God, you will find it is always worth it. Your bank account may take a hit and your calendar may need to be rearranged, but you will experience sweet joy through this act. This is how God's economy works.

PRACTICE REMINDER

Spend a few minutes praying
for an opportunity to serve
someone this week.

Day 2
Unexpected Servant

Read John 13:1–17.

The Passover Festival commemorates the first Passover (Exodus 12) when God instructed the Israelites, who were enslaved to Egypt, to paint the blood of a lamb over their doors. This signaled the Spirit of God to pass over that home and thus spare that family from his judgment. This act of judgment was how God released the Israelites from slavery. The Passover is full of rich symbolism that points to Jesus.

John tells us that it was just before the Passover Festival and Jesus knew he was entering the beginning of the end. He arranged for a place to share a meal with his disciples. The disciples didn't know it yet, but this would be their last meal together before Jesus's death. All the preparations for the meal had been made except one; there was no one to wash their feet.

Washing feet was more than just a hospitable gesture in this culture. Most people wore open-toed sandals and walked everywhere. The roads and walkways were dirty and dusty, traveled not just by people but by animals as well. All of this dust and muck would eventually find its way onto the feet of even the most conscientious walker. This combined with the fact that meals were traditionally served at low tables where guests would sit with their legs extended to the side or slightly behind themselves meant that washing feet was a necessity.

Foot washing was considered the most menial of tasks. It was work reserved for slaves and was usually given to the lowest ranking slave, which meant Gentile slaves did the work before Jewish ones. When there wasn't someone available to wash feet, most people usually did it themselves.

The disciples, however, didn't take the initiative to wash their own feet. They also didn't offer to wash each other's feet. Rather, they came in, sat down, and began to enjoy their meal. Jesus got up from the meal and took matters into his own hands as a way to teach the disciples and us some important lessons.

1. According to John 13:1–3, what did Jesus know to be true about himself? Considering his true identity, how do you think the disciples should have treated Jesus during the meal?

"We love until we are betrayed. Jesus continued to the cross despite betrayal. We love until we are forsaken. Jesus loved through forsakenness. We love up to a limit. Jesus loves to the end."[1]

—Dane Ortlund

2. Think about our world today and how we rank different kinds of work. What would you consider to be some of the more menial work there is to do today? How would you feel if you saw Jesus doing these jobs? How would you feel about doing one of these jobs yourself? Or if you regularly do one of these jobs, how do you feel about it? What are

some practical ways you can appreciate those who do these tasks?

John 13:3–4 tells us that because Jesus knew who he was, he was able to do something unexpected. Jesus got up, took off his outer garment, and wrapped a towel around his waist. This was the typical dress for a servant and thus, when Jesus did this, he was intentionally taking on the appearance of a servant or slave. Jesus, who should have been honored and served like a high-ranking king, took on the posture of the lowest of the low.

3. Just like Jesus understood who he was, it's important for us to know who we truly are in him. Read the following verses and circle all the things that are true about you as a follower of Jesus.

   "So in Christ Jesus you are all children of God through faith. . . . There is neither Jew nor Gentile, neither slave nor free, nor is there male and female, for you are all one in Christ Jesus." (Galatians 3:26, 28)

   "But our citizenship is in heaven." (Philippians 3:20)

   "For we are God's handiwork, created in Christ Jesus to do good works, which God prepared in advance for us to do." (Ephesians 2:10)

   "So God created mankind in his own image, in the image of God he created them; male and female he created them." (Genesis 1:27)

"But you are a chosen people, a royal priesthood, a holy nation, God's special possession, that you may declare the praises of him who called you out of darkness into his wonderful light." (1 Peter 2:9)

Is there one characteristic from these verses that stands out to you above the others? If so, what makes it meaningful to you?

Are there any other truths about your identity in Christ that you would add to the list?

Is there anything on this list that you struggle to believe is true of you? If so, why do you think that is?

"The LORD does not look at the things people look at. People look at the outward appearance, but the LORD looks at the heart."
—1 Samuel 16:7

4. What work do you do that you feel isn't valued or is often overlooked by others? How can remembering and then resting in your true identity help you change your approach to this work? What are some practical ways you can remind yourself what is true about who you are when you begin to feel frustrated by these tasks?

5. John 13 seems to indicate that all of the disciples besides Peter were silent, or at least didn't protest, when Jesus washed their feet. We have no idea what they were thinking, but considering what you know about foot washing in this culture, what do you think they might have been thinking? What might you have been thinking?

Peter, unlike the rest of the disciples, speaks up and questions what Jesus is doing. This is the third time we've seen Peter speak out in what could be considered a bit impulsive. The first time was when Peter rebuked Jesus for talking about his coming death (Mark 8:31–33) and Jesus immediately rebuked him by saying, "Get behind me, Satan." The second time was on the Mount of Transfiguration (Mark 9:5–6) when he spoke out of fear and ignorance and offered to build three shelters. And now this would be the third time.

Peter seemed to be a master at speaking before he thought things all the way through. I think Peter's bold use of his words is both a gift and a hindrance. It is a gift in that Peter was brave enough to state truth when others were silent. As we will see, God used this boldness in Peter's life to preach the gospel even when Peter was faced with real danger. However, it can also be a hindrance when left unchecked. Peter needed to learn when to speak and when to be silent. God was teaching Peter how to use his words well. It's not something just Peter needed to learn; it's something we need to learn too.

6. How do you resonate with Peter and his tendency to speak without thinking things through? Think about a recent time when you did this. What compelled you to speak out? How was it received? Is there anything you would do differently if you were placed in the same situation again? On the flip side, if you tend to be more naturally reserved in speaking out, how could you learn from Peter and choose to be more bold in how you use your words?

Spend a few minutes praying for an
opportunity to serve someone this week.

Day 3
You Are Clean

Review John 13:1–17.

Jesus used the lowly act of washing the disciples' feet as an opportunity to teach a deeper lesson about being spiritually cleansed.

7. Jesus implied there were two kinds of washing in this passage. What were they (John 13:10)? What do you think they represent?

8. Look up the following passages and summarize what they say about how we are made clean before God.

Romans 3:22–24

Ephesians 2:8–9

2 Corinthians 5:21

A few terms in these verses can be confusing. First is *righteous* or *righteousness*. These terms simply mean we have been made right in God's eyes. *Righteousness* is best understood when combined with the second term, *justification*. Justification "is a judicial act of God, by which he pardons all the sins of those who believe in Christ, and accounts, accepts, and treats them as righteous in the eye of the law."[2] We are made righteous because we are justified through Christ.

When we come to have faith in Jesus, we are made righteous once and for all. It is not something we have to earn or something we have to fight to keep. It is a gift given to us because of Jesus. We cannot lose our righteous standing because Jesus cleared our sin debt.

9. Knowing that you are made righteous through your faith in Christ, look up the following passages and write what they say about what we are supposed to do with the ongoing sin in our lives.

   Matthew 6:9–13. (Note: This is often called the Lord's Prayer and is the prayer that Jesus taught the disciples [and us] to pray. Pay special attention to verse 12. *Debt* can also be translated as "sin.")

1 John 1:8–10

10. Having considered the verses in questions 8 and 9, what do you think Jesus meant when he said, "Those who have had a bath need only to wash their feet; their whole body is clean" (John 13:10)?

11. Repentance is the act of confessing and turning from our ongoing sin to God. We do this with full assurance that we are forgiven. Take a moment to reflect on your past few days and ask God to make you aware of places where you sinned. Write down what comes to mind. Feel free to write in code or fold over the page once you're finished.

Now take a few minutes to pray and confess these specific things to God, telling him you are sorry for how you chose to sin and asking him to help you make different choices moving forward. Finally, take a moment to rest in knowing that you are fully forgiven.

PRACTICE REMINDER

Spend a few minutes praying for an
opportunity to serve someone this week.

Day 4
Do As I Have Done

Read John 13:12–17.

Jesus put on his regular clothes and returned to his place at the
table. He then asked the disciples if they understood what he had
done for them. With this question, Jesus moved into a second
lesson for the disciples.

12. Read Luke 22:24–27. Luke records different details of the
    Last Supper, and in this set of verses the disciples entered
    into a dispute. Many scholars believe this probably hap-
    pened just prior to the foot washing. What were the disci-
    ples arguing about?

    Compare this with John 13:14–16. What does Jesus say
    about how God views greatness? How do you think the
    disciples felt about this teaching of Jesus after they had just
    been disputing their rankings?

13. Ultimately, Jesus said the foot washing was an example
    that we should follow (John 13:15). What could it look like
    for us to wash feet today? What did he say would happen
    if we follow his example (verse 17)? What do you think
    this means? How have you experienced this truth when you
    have engaged in humble service?

14. Read John 13:2 and 11 again, followed by Matthew 5:43–
    44. As we will study in day 5, Judas is the one who will
    betray Jesus. Do you think Jesus skipped washing Judas's
    feet? Why or why not? What are the implications for us?

15. Prayerfully ask God if he wants you to serve someone you
    might consider an enemy. What do you think he wants you
    to do? Consider sharing this with your group for account-
    ability and prayer.

Some of us have enemies whom it would be emotionally damaging or otherwise dangerous for us to serve—for example, someone who has been abusive. As you pray about whether you have an enemy you should serve, know that the Lord does not desire you to subject yourself to further abuse. If a person or situation comes to mind that has been harmful to you, please talk to a professional counselor or a pastor to help you discern what you are really being called to do. Perhaps the act of serving and loving that you are called to is releasing and forgiving from afar.

16. Think of a time when you were in need and others served you. What happened? How was their act of humble service a blessing to you? If you've never told them, consider sending them a note or text to let them know how this act blessed you.

Spend a few minutes praying for an
opportunity to serve someone this week.

Day 5
Fighting Betrayal

Read John 13:18–30.

After the lessons taught through the foot washing, Jesus told his
disciples that one of them would betray him.

17. According to verse 19, why does Jesus tell them what is go-
    ing to happen? This phrase, "I AM WHO I AM," would have
    been familiar to the disciples. Read Exodus 3:14–15, which
    is when God reveals himself to Moses. What is Jesus clearly
    claiming to be true about who he really is?

18. How does verse 21 describe Jesus's demeanor? It's clear that
    Jesus knew Judas would betray him before it happened.
    Why then do you think it had this kind of impact on Jesus?
    What do you think this means about how Jesus felt about
    Judas? What do you think this says about how Jesus feels
    about us even when we choose to sin?

19. How did the disciples react to the news that one of them would betray Jesus (see verse 22 and Matthew 26:22)? Why do you think this news made them react in these ways? Consider all the ways they reacted: confused, sad, and questioning if they would be the one to betray Jesus.

20. Specifically, why do you think each of them wondered if he might be the one who would betray Jesus? Thinking of your own life and the ways you are tempted to sin, how do you relate to their question?

21. Read Hebrews 4:14–16. What does this passage state about how fully Jesus understands what we are going through when we feel weak or tempted? What should we do when this happens (verse 16)? Take a few minutes right now to "approach God's throne" about one of the ways you feel tempted to choose something other than what he would say is best (for example: giving in to your anger, overindulging, taking what isn't yours, thinking thoughts you shouldn't, etc.). Ask him for his grace and mercy to help you. Then write down a few practical ways you can choose God's way instead of this temptation to sin and commit to trusting God to help you do this.

A common question about Judas's betrayal is, did he have a choice in the matter? The short answer is he always had a choice, just like we do. God didn't make Judas sin. But God knew Judas would sin. This is hard for us to understand because we move through time differently than God does. God lives outside of time, so he sees past, present, and future all at once. Because of this, God knew the choice Judas would make. When Judas took the bread from Jesus, the text tells us that Satan entered Judas (John 13:27). This meant that Judas had fully and finally given himself over to the plans of the Enemy and was now acting on his behalf.

Judas left. Only Jesus really understood why. This set in motion the final stages of God's plan to rescue us, his beloved people.

While Judas gave himself over to the Enemy's plan, rest assured that we do not have to. No matter what kind of temptation you may be facing, if you go boldly to God, he promises to give you his grace and mercy to help you in your time of need (Hebrews 4:16). This is a bold promise you can cling to. Again and again.

22. Look back over this week's readings and capture the discipleship lessons you think Peter learned. The main discipleship lessons I think Peter learned were:

23. Flip back through all of week 5, including the practice section, and prayerfully ask the Lord to help you notice what he wants you to take away. Ask yourself questions like: Did I learn something new? Do I feel like God is inviting me to trust or follow him in a new way? Is there a change I need to make? Or is there something else he seems to be drawing my attention to?

My takeaways are:

Matthew tells us that at the end of the meal, Jesus and the disciples sang a hymn together (Matthew 26:30). Tradition informs us that this hymn would have been taken from Psalms 115–118.

I've often wondered what it would have been like to stand in the upper room and worship with Jesus and the disciples after all they had just experienced. Did they sing softly in solemn reverence because they knew the road ahead was about to get difficult, or did they stand to their feet and sing loudly as a way to proclaim victory in spite of what was coming? We don't know, but we can be sure that these words provided needed encouragement for all of them, especially Jesus who was headed into his last hours before his death.

PRACTICE REFLECTION

1. Write about someone you were able to serve this week. What happened?

2. Jesus stated in John 13:17 that we would be blessed by serving others. Did serving someone bless you in any way? If so, how?

3. Did you learn anything new about God or yourself through this experience? If so, what?

MISSING THE MARK

Day 1

Practice: Praying for God's Will

It's been years now, but I still remember the feeling of desperation and exhaustion like it was yesterday. I was truly running on empty. I had a fussy infant, a job that was deeply unfulfilling, a husband who was overextended due to graduate work, and barely enough money to put food on the table. I knew I couldn't keep going with circumstances as they were—something needed to change. And so, I prayed the same prayer I had been praying for months: "Lord, please do something. Please fix this. But please don't make us sell our house."

Oh, you see the problem with that prayer, don't you?

I wanted God's help, but I wanted it on my terms. When you really boil it down, I wanted something more than I wanted God. Being years removed from the situation, I see just how much stress and anxiety I caused by fighting to hold on to something the Lord was asking me to let go of. I don't want to minimize the situation we were in—giving up the place I called home was a big deal. Giving up anything we truly love is a big deal.

The Lord allowed me to stay in this place of desperation until I was willing to release everything to him. He wanted so much more for me, but first I needed to surrender to his will above my own. I eventually got there. We sold the house, I quit my job, and we moved into a friend's unfinished basement. I started to breathe again, and my joy began to return. I discovered that home wasn't just found in that little house; it could also be in an unfinished basement. In fact, for the two years we lived there, that little basement became more my home than the house had been.

This experience became a master class in God's goodness and grace. I learned that when I prayed prayers that truly surrendered to his will, he did things that were both different and better than I could ever imagine. (Isaiah 55:8–9 and Ephesians 3:20 reinforce these truths.)

This type of prayer is sometimes called a *prayer of indifference*. The term *indifference* used in the context of prayer is credited to Ignatius of Loyola, a Spanish priest in the sixteenth century. He taught that indifference doesn't mean we don't care about the outcome but that we are unconcerned, or indifferent, to anything except the will of God. When indifferent, we can boldly lay our requests before God and then trust him with whatever answer he sends.

Peter Scazzero writes of prayers of indifference,

> Arriving at this place of interior indifference and trusting that God's will is good—no matter the outcome—is no small task. We are attached to all kinds of secondary things—titles, positions, honors, places, persons, security, and the opinion of others. When these attachments are excessive, they become disordered attachments, or disordered loves, that push God out of the center of our life and become the core of our identity.[1]

This statement is so very true. When I was holding on to our home with a white-knuckled grip, I was more identified with the safety, status, and ideals it provided than with being God's child and wanting what he wanted. It wasn't until I reordered my loves and put God back in his rightful place that I was able to accept his will ahead of my own. The process wasn't easy. And I've had to go through this process many times. It turns out that houses aren't the only thing I can allow to become a disordered love in my life.

This week, we are going to practice trusting in God's goodness and grace by praying with indifference—boldly and specifically laying our requests before God and then asking the Lord to help us loosen our grip so we can echo Jesus's words, "yet not as I will, but as you will."

To do this, choose one thing you have been asking the Lord for or seeking his leading on. Write out a brief prayer naming what you specifically desire. Then pause and with intentionality write, "yet not as I will, but as you will." Sit quietly in the Lord's presence for a moment and rest in your surrender to him. As you do, remember who he is and how much he loves you. Remember that he is good and has the best for you. If you aren't ready to be fully surrendered and indifferent to the outcome quite yet, then start with, "Lord, help me get to the place where I can say 'yet not as I will, but as you will.'" Every day before you begin your lesson, pray your written prayer and then rest in God's love for you.

Write your prayer of indifference here:

Before you start your lesson, pray your prayer of
indifference and then rest in God's love for you.

Day 2
Sleeping Instead of Praying

Read Matthew 26:31–46.

This passage picks up just after the Passover meal and the foot
washing that we studied in the last lesson. After Jesus and the eleven
remaining disciples left the upper room, they headed toward the
Mount of Olives. The Mount of Olives is just outside of Jerusalem;
as the name suggests, it is an elevated spot that is full of olive trees.
On this small mountain there was a private garden (the garden of
Gethsemane) that Jesus frequented with his disciples (John 18:2).

As you just read in the passage, somewhere along the journey
to the garden, Jesus told the disciples that they would all abandon him. I imagine they were all a little offended. Jesus was their
beloved teacher and rabbi. And each disciple had left behind family, friends, and livelihoods to follow him. They had all paid a
great price to be on this journey. Why would they walk away now?

Peter, true to form, was the one who spoke up. He declared,
"Even if all fall away on account of you, I never will" (Matthew
26:33). I wonder how these words landed with the others. But we
don't get to know what the others were thinking or even what
their side conversations were; we just get to hear the conversation
between Jesus and Peter. And Jesus was adamant that it would
happen just like he said. He then added that a rooster would
crow twice just after Peter denied him.

Peter once again declared that even if he had to die with Jesus,
he wouldn't disown him. Finally, we hear from the others, and
they all agree with Peter that they won't walk away either.

This important passage sets up our lesson. Peter's confidence was sorely misplaced, and he and the others failed, just like Jesus said they would.

Before we move on from this set-up passage, I want you to notice Jesus's words in verse 32, "But after I have risen, I will go ahead of you into Galilee." I see so much grace and hope in these words. In the midst of telling them that they would stumble and experience failure, he was making sure they knew that they would also be restored. By stating that he would go ahead of them to Galilee, he implied that he would meet them there. Their failures would not be a sad end to this epic journey. There would be additional opportunities for them to learn how to truly be his disciples.

After this conversation ended, Jesus told the disciples to sit and wait while he went to pray. He then took Peter, James, and John farther into the garden.

1. What emotions did Jesus begin to experience (Matthew 26:37–38)? Why do you think Jesus was experiencing such intense emotions? What did he ask Peter, James, and John to do for him? Why do you think he did this?

Jesus stated that his soul was "overwhelmed with sorrow to the point of death" (Matthew 26:38). He was using the Greek word *psuche*, translated as soul, which means a person's entire being. Jesus's entire being was consumed with these emotions because he was wrestling through what was coming. Jesus, who was without sin, was preparing to take on the full weight and burden of humanity's sin. Although we can't even begin to grasp this kind of distress, we can identify partially with his emotions because we know something of grief, sorrow, and trouble.

2. Next to each verse, write a summary of what happened.

Jesus's first prayer (verse 39)

Jesus returned (verses 40–41)

Jesus's second prayer (verse 42)

Jesus returned (verse 43)

Jesus's third prayer (verse 44)

Jesus returned (verses 45–46)

What do you notice about how Jesus prayed? Why do you think the disciples kept falling asleep? How do you think Peter felt when Jesus called him out for failing to stay awake and keep watch?

3. Read Matthew 26:41 again. The word Jesus used for "spirit" in verse 41 is *pneuma*, which is referring to the Holy Spirit. The word he used for "flesh" is *sarx*, which refers to the part of our human nature that is prone to sin. What temptation do you think Jesus was concerned about them falling into? (Consider Matthew 26:31–35 among other things you think they might have been tempted to do.)

4. Read the passages below and underline what the Spirit is "willing" to do.

"In the same way, the Spirit helps us in our weakness. We do not know what we ought to pray for, but the Spirit himself intercedes for us through wordless groans." (Romans 8:26)

"And I will ask the Father, and he will give you another advocate to help you and be with you forever—the Spirit of truth. The world cannot accept him, because it neither sees him nor knows him. But you know him, for he lives with you and will be in you." (John 14:16–17)

"So I say, walk by the Spirit, and you will not gratify the desires of the flesh. For the flesh desires what is contrary to the Spirit, and the Spirit what is contrary to the flesh. They are in conflict with each other, so that you are not to do whatever you want." (Galatians 5:16–17)

5. Where have you noticed this conflict between your flesh and the Spirit in your own life recently? Have you ever successfully overcome temptation or weakness as a result of praying and depending on the Spirit? If so, describe what happened. How can you depend on the Spirit for the conflict you just identified?

Jesus, in the midst of his indescribable grief and turmoil, came back to the disciples and after finding them asleep didn't give them a lecture on how selfish or shortsighted they were. Rather, he encouraged them to wake up to pray for themselves so that *they* wouldn't fall into temptation. In his dark hour where he needed his friends the most, Jesus still saw what *they* needed even more.

Jesus was teaching Peter and the others that depending on the Spirit through prayer is fundamental to discipleship. As Christians, we all know we should pray, yet many of us have dry prayer lives. To be honest, we would rather do what Peter did—sleep instead of pray. I think this is because somewhere along the way we bought the lie that our prayers don't really matter. But even when the answer is no, our prayers still have an impact.

6. Even though God the Father did not grant Jesus's request, what does Luke 22:43–44 tell us happened as a result of Jesus's prayers? Have you ever prayed for something fervently and not received the answer you desired? What happened? Did you notice any benefit to your relationship with God or your ability to trust him as a result of the prayers?

"In the first garden 'Not your will but mine' changed Paradise to desert and brought man from Eden to Gethsemane. Now 'Not my will but yours' brings anguish to the man who prays it but transforms the desert into the kingdom and brings man from Gethsemane to the gates of glory."[2]

—D. A. Carson

Before you start your lesson, pray your prayer of
indifference and then rest in God's love for you.

Day 3
Futile Fighting

Read Matthew 26:47–56.

As we read yesterday, Jesus was in such deep anguish that he
started to sweat drops of blood (Luke 22:44). Science tells us that
only the most extreme stress can cause someone to sweat blood.
Jesus was under this kind of stress because he knew what was
coming. He returned to the sleepy three and collected the rest of
the group, telling them it was time to go because the betrayer,
Judas, had arrived.

Judas showed up with an army beside him. It seems they expected
a fight from Jesus and the eleven remaining disciples. This is more
proof that they didn't know who Jesus was or what he had come to
do. Jesus wasn't there to set up a temporary kingdom through power
and might, but an eternal kingdom through sacrifice and death.

Judas greeted Jesus and kissed him. This was the secret signal.

7. Imagine this scene. It is well into the night and an army is
   marching toward Jesus and the disciples. Jesus isn't putting
   up a fight, but the men still seem aggressive. Peter grabs his
   sword and tries to defend Jesus (see John 18:10–11). Why
   do you think Peter did this? According to Luke 22:51, what
   did Jesus do next?

8. Compare Matthew 16:21–23 with Peter's actions in this passage. What similarities do you see? What does it seem like Peter was trying to do? Why do you think he was still responding like this?

"Had Jesus not healed the ear of Malchus, there probably would have been *four* crosses on Calvary!"[3]
—Warren Wiersbe

9. Reflecting on the prayer you wrote in the practice section, how might you be tempted to act in ways similar to Peter and either try to take matters into your own hands or attempt to help God along in getting the answer you desire? Knowing that there are also times when God does call us to action, what are some ways you have discovered that help you know when it is time to act versus time to wait?

10. Look up the following verses and write what Jesus told the disciples in each passage.

Matthew 16:21

Matthew 17:22–23

Matthew 20:17–19

Matthew 26:2

Why do you think Peter and the others were still resistant to Jesus's arrest? Do you think they hadn't heard what Jesus had been saying or do you think there was another reason?

Jesus reprimanded Peter for his actions and told the disciple that he could call down an army from heaven if needed. But Jesus wouldn't, because everything that was happening was to fulfill God's better plan (Matthew 26:54).

When Jesus referred to the Scriptures (verse 54) and the writings of the prophets (verse 56), he was referring to prophecies that were written down about him in what we now refer to as the Old Testament. Jesus fulfilled numerous prophecies with his birth, life, death, and resurrection. Depending on the process used for counting, some number them upwards of three hundred. No matter how you count, though, there are many, many prophecies that Jesus directly fulfilled. This is just more evidence that he is the one of whom the Scriptures foretold.

11. According to Matthew 26:56, the disciples deserted Jesus and fled. Why do you think they did this after they had just declared they wouldn't?

12. Have you ever been in a situation where you knew something you didn't want to happen was going to happen (for example: a job loss you suspected was coming, an illness that led to the death of a loved one, a rejection you felt to be inevitable, a relationship ending, etc.)? Even though you knew this hard thing would probably happen, how did you respond in the moment when it actually happened? Does this help you understand why Peter and the others may have responded as they did and if so, how?

While Jesus had been clear with the disciples about what was coming, their reactions show that they weren't able to really receive what he had been telling them. They filtered his words through their expectations and desires. We do this too. We love to rest in God's promises of abundance (John 10:10), while overlooking the simultaneous truth that there will be times of trials and troubles for all believers (John 16:33). Both are true and we need to expect both experiences. If we only expect blessing, trials will become overly disruptive to our fragile faith. I think this is one of the main reasons the disciples fled—they became disoriented by their dashed expectations and didn't know what else to do.

Before you start your lesson, pray your prayer of indifference and then rest in God's love for you.

Day 4
Weakness Exposed

Read Matthew 26:57–58, 69–75.

After Jesus's arrest, the disciples scattered and fled the scene, but Peter didn't seem to go far; he followed Jesus at a distance into the courtyard of the high priest. I feel a little hopeful for Peter in this moment. He hadn't completely deserted Jesus. Maybe there's still a chance he can hold strong. But this is a false hope, since we know the prediction Jesus made about Peter will certainly, and sadly, happen. It was evening, and it must have been chilly because Mark 14:67 tells us Peter warmed himself by the fire. It was here, in the glow of the flames, that Peter was called out.

13. Using these passages from Matthew 26, fill in the table with who spoke to Peter, what they said, and how he responded.

Verses	Who spoke to Peter?	What did they say?	How did Peter respond?
69–70			
71–72			
73–74			

What do you notice about Peter's responses?

14. What fears do you have about people finding out you're associated with Jesus? What do you do as a result of these fears? Is there something you can do differently to help you combat these fears?

15. Immediately after Peter disowned Jesus the third time, the rooster crowed. What detail does Luke 22:61 add? What do you think was the look on Jesus's face?

Peter heard the rooster and looked into the eyes of Jesus. At that moment, he seemed overcome by the realization of what he'd done. He turned and went outside, where he wept bitterly.

16. What do you think Peter was thinking and feeling as he "wept bitterly"?

The very next passage (Matthew 27:1–5) tells of Judas being overcome with remorse for his act of betrayal. These accounts, back-to-back in Scripture, highlight Peter's and Judas's vastly different reactions to their betrayals. Peter was heartbroken over what he'd done. He grieved over his sin and I'm sure he wished he could have done it differently, but even in that terrible moment he still knew he was deeply loved by Jesus. Jesus had told him this truth over and over again. Not to mention that Jesus had told Peter and the other disciples this exact thing would happen and had already made a way for their restoration (Matthew 26:32). Judas, on the other hand, also saw he'd done something terrible and even tried to undo his actions by returning the money. But Judas became consumed by what he had done and couldn't see a way out. The difference between them was that Peter knew who Jesus really was and Judas didn't. This allowed Peter to cling to hope. Judas, however, lost all hope and took his own life.

Peter experienced conviction, which is from God and leads us to repentance and restoration. Judas experienced being consumed by shame, which is a tactic of the Enemy to lead us to self-loathing and hopelessness. As God's children, when we sin, we should experience godly conviction that leads to repentance and restoration. We should not experience all-consuming shame, because nothing we do or don't do can ever separate us from the love of God (Romans 8:38–39).

17. When have you experienced deep conviction due to sin in your life? What happened? How did you work through the emotions? (If you need a reminder that you are fully and finally forgiven through Jesus's death and resurrection, reflect back to day 3 in lesson 5, starting on page 106.) If you haven't experienced this kind of conviction, why do you think that is?

Before you start your lesson, pray your prayer of
indifference and then rest in God's love for you.

Day 5
An Antidote to Sin

Yes, Peter denied Jesus just like Jesus said he would. But this
wasn't Peter's only failure. He also fell asleep when Jesus asked
him to stay awake. And he nearly started a war when Jesus said
he should just stand by. These three failures, stacked one on
another, must have left Peter feeling deeply discouraged. After
all, how could Peter, the rock, have let these things happen?

It seemed Peter believed he was stronger and more capable than
he really was. His self-image was bloated by pride. In the end all
it took was some physical exhaustion, being impassioned by his
ideas, and the questions of a young servant girl with no status
to make him crumble. Sometimes God uses our brokenness and
our failures to help us truly change the way we do things. This is
exactly what he did with Peter.

Jesus had significant work for Peter to do once he had ascended
into heaven—work that the gospel message depended on. And
if Peter remained dependent upon
himself, puffed up with pride, then he
would have been ineffective at the real
work God was inviting him to do. Peter
needed to become indifferent to what
he wanted and surrendered to what
God wanted instead. This is the crux
of humility, and for Peter it came about
when he hit the bottom and learned
that his way was not *the* way.

"Pride is spiritual can-
cer: it eats up the very
possibility of love, or
contentment, or even
common sense."[4]
— C. S. Lewis

For us to be effective in the work God is inviting us to do, we also need to learn these lessons.

18. After Jesus's death and resurrection, Peter wrote two letters that reflected on and taught some of what he had learned in his journey with Jesus. Read his words below from 1 Peter. Circle each use of *humility* or *humble*.

"All of you, clothe yourselves with humility toward one another, because, 'God opposes the proud but shows favor to the humble.' Humble yourselves, therefore, under God's mighty hand, that he may lift you up in due time. Cast all your anxiety on him because he cares for you. Be alert and of sober mind. Your enemy the devil prowls around like a roaring lion looking for someone to devour. Resist him, standing firm in the faith." (1 Peter 5:5–9)

How would you define *godly humility*? (Use a dictionary and this verse to help you.) How is godly humility the antithesis of pride?

19. According to 1 Peter 5:5–9, write out the characteristics of God versus your Enemy the devil. What part does this enemy play in trying to keep you from living with humility? How have you seen this play out in your life, even in the last few weeks?

20. One way to defeat the Enemy is to choose to grow in humility. Read the following passages and briefly summarize how they say we can embody humility (or simply underline it if it's explicit in the verse).

"Do nothing out of selfish ambition or vain conceit. Rather, in humility value others above yourselves, not looking to your own interests but each of you to the interests of the others." (Philippians 2:3–4)

"The LORD has told you what is good, and this is what he requires of you: to do what is right, to love mercy, and to walk humbly with your God." (Micah 6:8 NLT)

"Do not conform to the pattern of this world, but be transformed by the renewing of your mind. Then you will be able to test and approve what God's will is—his good, pleasing and perfect will. For by the grace given me I say to every one of you: Do not think of yourself more highly than you ought, but rather think of yourself with sober judgment, in accordance with the faith God has distributed to each of you." (Romans 12:2–3)

"Humble yourselves before God. Resist the devil, and he will flee from you. Come close to God, and God will come close to you." (James 4:7–8 NLT)

Pause and prayerfully ask God to draw your attention to one of the summaries or underlined phrases from the above

passages. Place a star by the one that seems to stand out
the most. What is one practical thing you can do this week
to help you move toward the thing that you placed a star
by? How might this help you combat the Enemy's tactics in
your life?

21. Peter had to learn to be indifferent to anything but God's
will. Reflecting on this lesson, write out three ways you
saw Peter act in ways that brought about his own ideas and
will ahead of God's. Next to this, write what you imagine
could have happened differently if Peter had been truly indifferent to anything but God's will in these circumstances.
Underline which one would have been better. How does
this encourage you to choose God's will over your own?

1.

2.

3.

22. Look back over this week's readings and capture the discipleship lessons you think Peter learned. The main discipleship lessons I think Peter learned were:

23. Flip back through week 6, including the practice section, and prayerfully ask the Lord to help you notice what he wants you to take away from this lesson. Ask yourself questions like: Did I learn something new? Do I feel like God is inviting me to trust or follow him in a new way? Is there a change I need to make? Or is there something else he seems to be drawing my attention to?

My takeaways are:

I've been in a season of earnestly seeking the Lord's will for my life. As I shared earlier in the study, God has led me to make a significant change in my life by leaving my career in pastoral ministry. When he started nudging my heart with this idea, I started seeking him in earnest prayer specifically about this. I want to be honest and tell you that prayers of indifference have been difficult for me in this season. There are a lot of things I desire in my life, and while many of them are good, they are not all God's best for me. I have had to continually remind myself that what I want more than anything is God's will, even when it doesn't make sense to me.

This verse from the book of Isaiah has been helpful to me:

"'For my thoughts are not your thoughts, neither are your ways my ways,' declares the Lord. 'As the heavens are higher than the earth, so are my ways higher than your ways and my thoughts than your thoughts.'" (Isaiah 55:8–9)

This verse combined with who I know God to be reminds me that I can trust him. A lot of time things don't make sense in the moment—like selling a house or leaving a career. And yet when these things are God's will, we can trust that he is working them out for our good and his glory (Romans 8:28–29 and Ephesians 2:10).

Peter learned through some difficult circumstances that God's plan was better than his, just like how we often have to learn these lessons. And even when Peter stumbled, Jesus was right there to help him up. Jesus never turned his back on Peter; instead, he gently taught him what he needed to know.

If you are feeling discouraged by how hard it is to pray with indifference or how often you stumble, then let me encourage you that Jesus is there to help you too. He is always ready and always willing to help us refocus and continue the journey. Don't give up, my friend. God has good plans for you, just like he had for Peter. Just like he has for me. And his plans are always the best plans. May we be indifferent to anything else.

PRACTICE REFLECTION

1. As you sought to pray with indifference this week, did you notice anything happen regarding this prayer (for example, maybe a specific answer or something that happened in your own heart)?

2. Did you learn anything new about God or yourself through your attempt to pray with indifference? If so, what did you learn?

REPENTANCE AND RENEWAL

Day 1
Practice: Prayers of Repentance

No one is perfect. We all have our moments. We get angry when we should be patient. We say things we wish we could simply rewind and say differently. We are selfish when we should be generous. To be honest, sometimes we have no idea why we do the things we do—since they are the exact opposite of what we really wanted to do in the first place. I resonate with the words of Paul, "I do not understand what I do. For what I want to do I do not do, but what I hate to do I do" (Romans 7:15). Anyone else?

All of these failures are really sin—small, big, and everywhere in between. They happen in our lives just like they happened in Peter's life. They are moments when we allow our will and desires to become bigger and more important than God's perfect will. The good news is that just like Jesus restored Peter after his failures, he longs to do the same for us.

Even better news is that none of our sin failures can ever remove us from God's love, grace, and forgiveness. Our eternal relationship and right standing with him are secure because of

Jesus's death and resurrection (Romans 8:1–2). This is something theologians call eternal security, and it is a beautiful truth that we can stand on. Once we choose to have faith in Jesus, there is nothing we can do that will ever separate us from his love and acceptance (Romans 8:38–39).

And yet, while all this is true, Scripture still tells us that when we sin, we need to confess and repent of that sin. (As a reminder, we studied this in lesson 5 when Jesus told Peter that only his feet needed to be washed because the rest of him was clean. You can review the concept there as well as in 1 John 1:9 and Matthew 6:9–13.)

Repentance means we recognize where we have been wrong; we turn away from that sin and turn back to God. Said another way, repentance is agreeing with God about our sin and choosing his way over our way. Notice that repenting is more than just saying we are sorry for what we have done. True repentance implies both a change in heart and a change in action. We know this is true from our own life experience. If someone tells us they are sorry for something and then keeps repeating the same hurtful actions, we know they really aren't all that sorry.

This week we are going to spend time reflecting on where we have chosen our ways over God's ways and then pray earnest prayers of repentance and ask him to help us to do things differently moving forward. I will walk you through this process, but before we begin, I'd like to add a note of caution: Beware of the Enemy. The Enemy is called the "father of lies" (John 8:44) for good reason. I've seen two ways he tries to lie to us in this practice. The first is by trying to convince us that our sin is really no big deal. This lie sounds something like, "You've already been forgiven, so why do you need to even try to live differently? After all, it doesn't really matter." (See Romans 6:1–2.)

This lie not only cheapens what Jesus did on the cross for us, but also keeps us limping along in bondage to our broken and sinful ways. Jesus clearly stated that he came to bring us freedom from our sin, both now and in eternity, and through him we can live full and abundant lives (Galatians 5:1; John 10:10).

The second lying tactic the Enemy uses is on the other end of the spectrum. Here he beats us up with lies about who we are because of what we have done. This shame tactic tries to make us so identified with our sin that we can't see a way out of it. This is how the Enemy bested Judas. The Enemy may try to convince you that instead of just having an anger issue, you are an angry person through and through—it is who you are and there isn't anything you can do about it.

This is simply not true. The truth is the same as just stated above—Jesus came to bring freedom and abundant living both now and for eternity. We can find freedom from our sin through Jesus. But sometimes we do need help navigating a new way. If you are feeling consumed by a particular sin, seek out a trusted friend, pastor, or professional counselor to walk with you through this process.

Now that you know how to be on guard against the Enemy's tactics, let's get started. To begin, spend a few moments each day praying the following words from King David:

> Search me, O God, and know my heart;
> test me and know my anxious thoughts.
> Point out anything in me that offends you,
> and lead me along the path of everlasting life.
> —Psalm 139:23–24 (NLT)

Then ask the Lord to help you see what he wants you to notice. If nothing comes to mind right away, read and reflect on Galatians 5:22–23, which lists the characteristics we should have in our lives as followers of Jesus. These are called the fruit of the Spirit and they are love, joy, peace, patience, kindness, goodness, faithfulness, gentleness, and self-control. Slowly go through this list and ask the Lord to help you see where you failed to act in these ways over the last day or two.

When a situation comes to mind, agree with him about it and tell him you are sorry for what happened. Be specific and name what really happened and why. Take ownership of your part without justifying your actions based on the situation or what others did. While these may have contributed, you are still responsible for yourself. Then ask him to help you do it differently next time. If there is something you need to do to make it right, then find a way to do that quickly (for example, an apology to someone you were angry with). Finally, spend a few minutes resting in God's grace and love for you.

Take five minutes to do this practice now.

PRACTICE REMINDER

Spend a few minutes praying with
repentance as outlined in the practice.

Day 2
Reunited

Read Luke 24:1–16, 33–36.

Our last lesson ended with Peter realizing he had done exactly
what he said he would never do when three times he denied
knowing Jesus. Overcome by his actions, he went outside, away
from the sight of Jesus, and wept bitterly. My heart goes out to
Peter in this moment. He really thought he was stronger than
he was. And the realization that he rejected someone he loved
deeply in his moment of need brought deep regret. Peter's bitter
tears must have held pain, agony, and grief. I'm sure he wished he
could just get one more chance to go back and do it over.

At this point in the story Jesus was rapidly shuffled around
until he received an unjust conviction to be crucified. Jesus was
then beaten, marched up a hill, and hung on a cross. We, the
readers, are not terribly shocked by how these awful events
unfold because we knew it was coming. Peter and the rest of the
disciples, though, seemed caught off guard.

Sunday morning, three days after Jesus's death, Mary
Magdalene and some other female followers of Jesus (see Matthew 28:1; Mark 16:1; Luke 24:10; and John 20:1 for the different
women listed) set out to anoint Jesus's body with spices, an act of
love and honor to keep his decomposing body smelling fresh. The
women arrived to find his grave empty. Bewildered and fright-
ened, they encountered an angel who told them Jesus had risen.
Then they encountered Jesus himself, who told them to go and

tell the disciples to meet him in Galilee. (See Matthew 28:1–10; Mark 16:1–8; or Luke 24:1–10 to read about this account.)

As a woman, I pause every time I read this passage. Jesus chose women to be the first people he revealed himself to. He also chose these women to be his first evangelists, as they were the first people tasked to go and tell the good news about his resurrection.

Which also means Jesus relied on a group of women to initiate the entire gospel movement.

In his day, women were not regarded as reliable or trustworthy by the patriarchal society they lived in. Through Jesus's intentional actions, he went above and beyond to make sure we knew he valued and trusted women—just like men. This is our God. He is a God who values and uses everyone—even those the culture doesn't deem worthy. I wonder whom he would have chosen today?

Another thing to notice in these passages is that the angel calls Peter out by name. He told the women, "Go, tell his disciples and Peter" (Mark 16:7) that Jesus had gone ahead of them into Galilee, and they would see him there. The women went and told the others.

1. How do the disciples, besides Peter, react to the women's story (Luke 24:11)? If you had heard this news from them, what might you have thought? What do Peter and John do next (verse 12; John 20:3–4)? What do you think was going through Peter's mind as he ran to the tomb and then after he arrived?

At this point in the story, we need to dig a little deeper to piece together who Jesus saw and when. This is important because it helps us see when Peter got to interact with Jesus. We know Jesus saw the women at the tomb early on Sunday morning (Luke 24:1).

After that Luke tells us Jesus met with two other disciples, one named Cleopas and the other unnamed, on the road to Emmaus, where he explained the Scriptures to them (Luke 24:13–32). At the end of their conversation the two men immediately returned to Jerusalem, which was about seven miles away, to find the eleven disciples and the others who were with them. Considering travel time, it could have been no earlier than Sunday evening when Cleopas and this other disciple arrived in Jerusalem.

2. According to Luke 24:34, who else did Jesus appear to? (See also 1 Corinthians 15:3–5, where Peter is called Cephas.)

3. Scripture tells us that Peter and Jesus had this first private meeting but does not tell us what they discussed. What do you think Peter and Jesus talked about? Imagine if you were Peter, what do you think you would want to say to Jesus? And again, if you were Peter, is there anything you would hope Jesus would say or do during this meeting?

Of course, we have no idea what really transpired in this private meeting between Jesus and Peter, but many believe this was where Peter acknowledged his sin and asked Jesus to forgive him. If this happened, we have complete assurance that Jesus did forgive him.

4. Read and write a quick summary of the passages below. According to these verses, how do we know Jesus forgave Peter? How do you know he forgives you for your sins? Is there anything you struggle believing he can't forgive you for?

Psalm 103:10–12

Ephesians 1:7–8

1 John 1:9

As believers, we can rest in the full and complete forgiveness of our sins. When Jesus died on the cross, he took on all our sins through all of time. That means that more than two thousand years ago, Jesus died for your sins, and you weren't even born yet. Which means he also covered all the sins you still haven't committed yet. I know, it's a mind bender, but an amazing one. There is nothing you have done or can do that would make Jesus turn away from you. Read John 10:28–29 and Romans 8:38–39, if you need more assurance. There is nothing, absolutely nothing, you can do that would remove you from God's grace once you've received it.

Now that doesn't mean we shouldn't try to live a life that is honoring to God. We absolutely should. We seek this kind of life, though, because we trust and believe that the God who would die for us has our best interest at heart. This extravagant act reveals that his way is better than our way and we can rest in the truth that he is offering us a life full of freedom and abundance. We do not have to strive to live this way to earn his grace or favor, because it is freely given to us through our faith and not our actions (Ephesians 2:8–9).

5. Cleopas and the other disciple arrived in Jerusalem and told everyone else what had happened. Read Luke 24:33–37 and John 20:19. According to these verses, what do you think the atmosphere in the room was like? What do you think they were afraid of? What do you think you would have been afraid of?

6. Jesus greeted them and said, "Peace be with you." This is the second time Peter is recorded to have seen Jesus after his death and resurrection. In what ways do you think Peter and the others needed peace? What do you think it was like for Peter to see Jesus this second time?

7. Write down a few places where you need peace right now. Read Philippians 4:6–7, in the margin, and spend a few minutes praying about these things. Give them over to God, thank him for what is good, and then allow the peace of Christ to guard your heart and mind.

"Do not be anxious about anything, but in every situation, by prayer and petition, with thanksgiving, present your requests to God. And the peace of God, which transcends all understanding, will guard your hearts and your minds in Christ Jesus."
   —Philippians 4:6–7

If you are struggling to rest in and experience the peace of Christ in your life, take the time to do what this passage states. I've heard this passage called the prescription for peace, and it absolutely is. It's one of just a few places where we are given a promise that if we do what this passage states, peace will come. But we need to do all of it. So, start by spending time thanking God for what is good. I'd even recommend you make a list and post it somewhere you can see it. Gratitude goes a long way toward changing our hearts' natural inclination to stew in our anxieties. When we remind ourselves of what is good and true, worry is edged out. When it comes back, simply return to your list. Praise God again and lay what makes you anxious back at his feet. He will give you peace—over and over again. It's a promise.

Of course, if you are struggling with any form of clinical depression or anxiety, you may need additional help to find the peace that God has for you. If this is the case, I encourage you to seek out trained medical and mental health professionals. God has peace for you, but you may need some additional resources to find it. Keep going. God sees you and loves you.

Spend a few minutes praying with
repentance as outlined in the practice.

Day 3
A Lesson in Fishing

Read John 21:1–14.

Just before this passage we are studying today, John 20:24–29
tells us that Jesus appeared to the disciples "a week later." Once
again, they were behind locked doors, and Jesus stated, "Peace
be with you!" (John 20:26). We can only imagine how they
were feeling. Their leader had been brutally murdered and it
seems they were fearful they might be next. We can't really
blame them for locking the doors. We don't have many details
about this meeting, except that it was where Jesus helped his
disciple Thomas stop doubting that he had really been res-
urrected. While Peter is not mentioned by name, the passage
states that the disciples were there, so we can assume Peter was
included. This then would be the third recorded time Peter and
Jesus saw each other.

Since these interactions and times can start to get confusing, on
the next page there is a timeline for what we've looked at so far.

We don't know how much time passed between this encounter
and John 21. The text simply states it was "afterward." We know
that Jesus was on earth for forty days after his resurrection (Acts
1:3), so it couldn't have been too long, but it could have been a
week or more.

Peter and six other disciples were together by the Sea of Galilee,
and Peter declared that he was going to go fishing. The six who
were there joined him.

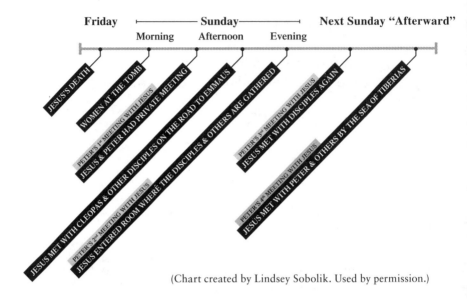

(Chart created by Lindsey Sobolik. Used by permission.)

8. Why do you think Peter went fishing? Based on his past, how could returning to this activity be comforting to him? What kinds of activities do you tend to gravitate to when you are in a season of waiting? Why do you think you choose to do these things? Do they help, hurt, or something else?

People have lots of thoughts on why Peter might have initiated this fishing excursion, but the truth is we don't really know. It could be that he was simply hungry or that he was trying to provide for himself and his family. Both seem like reasonable explanations. However, some people speculate that this fishing trip revealed something more about Peter. Namely, that he was still uncertain of his standing with Jesus and unsure of his usefulness moving forward. If this is the case, then Peter was reverting to what was known and was starting to be a fisher of fish instead of people (Luke 5:1–11). Sadly, he wasn't proving very successful at his old job.

9. If Peter did return to fishing because he was reverting to his previous life, why do you think he did this? What might he have struggled to believe was true about his usefulness to God moving forward? Is there anything you think Peter could have done that would have disqualified him from serving God moving forward? Do you think there is anything you could do, or have done, that would disqualify you from serving God?

There are different opinions on whether we can be disqualified from serving God in some capacity due to our sin. I land firmly in the camp that with God's grace and mercy, any sin we have committed can be overcome. However, it is possible that the specifics of our calling may need to change because of a sin (for example, if you embezzled money from your church, you probably won't be entrusted to manage money there again). But no matter what our past holds, we are always welcomed back into fellowship with Jesus. And, with the hard work of repentance and restoration, God will certainly have good work for us to do in the future. It may be in a different capacity than it would have been, but know that God is never done with you. Never. If you get nothing else from these next few days, notice the great lengths Jesus goes to to make sure Peter knows he is loved, forgiven, and restored.

10. There are a lot of similarities between this passage and the first miraculous catch of fish we studied a few weeks ago in Luke 5:4–11. Go back and read that passage, paying special attention to how Peter reacted to Jesus after the fish were

caught. Write down how Peter responded in each scenario. What do you think this second response says about Peter's heart toward Jesus now versus at the beginning of the journey?

First Catch	Second Catch

11. When Peter arrived on shore, what did he find (verse 9)? What does this mean that Jesus, the risen Lord, had been doing while the men were out fishing? How does this mimic what we learned about serving in lesson 5, when Jesus washed the disciples' feet at his last meal with them in the upper room (see also verse 13)?

12. Jesus was getting ready to have an important conversation with Peter. What did they do first (verse 12)? Why do you think this was important? Are there any principles you can learn from this encounter that could be applied to the next time you need to have an important conversation (even if it isn't centered around a meal)?

13. Compare John 21:9 with John 18:18, which describes Peter's denial of Jesus. What is similar about both of these scenes (consider the distinct smells and sounds)? Do you have a favorite meal from childhood? If so, what happens when you smell that meal today? Just like we get brought back to positive memories through smell, we can also be brought back to negative ones. What could this smell of wood burning bring Peter back to? What do you think Jesus might have been doing by recreating this similar atmosphere?

Spend a few minutes praying with
repentance as outlined in the practice.

Day 4
Restoration

Read John 21:15–18.

14. Jesus asked, "Simon, son of John, do you love me more
    than these?" What do you think "these" is referring to?
    Consider the three options below and place a star by what
    you think Jesus is asking.

    Do you love me more than you love these other men?

    Do you love me more than these men love me?

    Do you love me more than you love these things
    (fishing boat and career)?

    Read Matthew 26:33, which sets up the denial. What did
    Peter declare there? Does this shed any light on what Jesus
    might have meant by "these"?

15. Imagine you were having this conversation with Jesus. If Jesus asked you if you loved him more than "these," what are some things he could be referring to (list out people, possessions, roles, etc.)? How can these things get in the way of your serving Jesus wholeheartedly? Take a few minutes to prayerfully discuss this with God and if necessary repent of anything that may be distracting you or holding you back from being fully devoted to him. (Note that this doesn't necessarily mean we should just walk away from people or roles, but that we need to keep Jesus first.)

16. Jesus asked Peter nearly the same question three times, to which Peter gave nearly the same reply. After each question and reply Jesus exhorted Peter by using a metaphor to do something. Write those three things below. I've done the first one for you.

1. Feed my lambs

2.

3.

According to John 10:11, who is Jesus in this metaphor? Who are the sheep and lambs? And who do they belong to? What do you think Jesus was really asking Peter to do in feeding and caring for the sheep and lambs?

17. Reread what Jesus told Peter about his identity and calling in John 1:42 (recall that Cephas and Peter mean "rock"); Matthew 4:19; and Matthew 16:17–18. How was Jesus making sure Peter knew that his original calling had not changed? How do you think it felt for him to hear these truths again?

"God will not shame you into better behavior. He will not trick you. He will not tease you. He will not laugh at you. He will not terrorize you. He does not pull rugs out from under you. He does not drop the other shoe. He does not pull fast ones. He will not roll his eyes, throw up his hands, or turn his back on you."[1]
—Emily Freeman

18. Verse 17 says, "Peter was hurt because Jesus asked him the third time." Why do you think this wounded Peter? Do you think Jesus meant to wound Peter? Why or why not?

Jesus was confronting Peter about his disordered loves and reminding him of his calling. Although we won't get to have a beachside breakfast with Jesus when we need similar coaching, we do get the benefit of the Spirit who leads, guides, and convicts us. In our next lesson, we will spend some time reflecting on the role of the Spirit in our lives. For now, just know that if you feel any kind of conviction, it is with the same love and care that Jesus gave to Peter.

Day 5
Moving Forward

Read John 21:18–23.

The task of feeding and caring for the flock was not something
Peter was intended to carry alone. Jesus knew the number of
Christians would grow, and thus the care and feeding of his people would also grow and expand beyond Peter's capacity. Peter
would need to replicate himself by training, equipping, and
empowering others to help with this task.

Years later when Peter wrote his letters to the church, he
included this exhortation to leaders:

> "Care for the flock that God has entrusted to you. Watch
> over it willingly, not grudgingly—not for what you will
> get out of it, but because you are eager to serve God.
> Don't lord it over the people assigned to your care, but
> lead them by your own good example. And when the
> Great Shepherd appears, you will receive a crown of
> never-ending glory and honor." (1 Peter 5:2–4 NLT)

19. What stands out to you in this passage about how God's
    people should be cared for? How do you think these words
    echo what Jesus taught and exemplified to Peter? Give

examples from Peter's life, if possible. How and when is someone rewarded for this work?

20. Thinking of your own life, make a list based on the following prompts.

Who are some people that have "fed and cared" for me, and how did they do this?

Who are some people I have "fed and cared" for, and how did I do this?

Prayerfully ask God: Is there anyone you want me to "care for and feed" today? Write down any names that come to mind and ideas for how you could do this.

21. After Jesus told Peter how he would die, what did Jesus say next (John 21:19)? How did Peter react to this (verses 20–21)? Why do you think Peter did this?

It's incredibly tempting to compare our journey of following Jesus with others'. Is there anyone (or multiple people) whom you tend to compare your gifts and calling to? How does comparing yourself to this person or these people tend to affect you?

22. Paraphrase Jesus's response to Peter's question (verse 22).

Imagine Jesus is speaking these words over you in regard to the situation or person you identified in the last question. Take a moment to pray about this and then write what you think Jesus might say to you using the outline at the top of the next page.

For example, I could say: If I want Susie to sell millions of books, what is that to you? Jodie, you must follow me by being faithful to write what I'm calling you to write and shepherd the women I'm asking you to shepherd. (This is completely hypothetical, of course!)

If I want _____ to _____
_____, what is that to you? _____,
you must follow me by _____
_____

23. Look back over this week's readings and capture the disci-
    pleship lessons you think Peter learned. The main disciple-
    ship lessons I think Peter learned were:

24. Flip back through all of week 7, including the practice sec-
    tion, and prayerfully ask the Lord to help you notice what
    he wants you to take away from this lesson. Ask yourself
    questions like: Did I learn something new? Do I feel like
    God is inviting me to trust or follow him in a new way? Is
    there a change I need to make? Or is there something else
    he seems to be drawing my attention to?

    My takeaways are:

I hope you walk away from this lesson feeling deeply encouraged. Jesus was not done with Peter after his failure. Just like he is not done with me after my failures, and he is not done with you after yours either. No matter what someone may have told you, you have not and will not ever fall too far from his grace. Jesus is always ready and willing to forgive us and restore us.

If Peter's restoration doesn't convince you, consider this: Much of Scripture was written by murderers. Yes, I know that sounds crazy, but it's true. Moses wrote the first five books of the Bible and he murdered a man (Exodus 2:12); David wrote most of the Psalms and he committed both adultery and murder (2 Samuel 11:14–15); and Paul wrote a good percentage of the New Testament and prior to his conversion, he actively persecuted and oversaw the murder of believers (Acts 7:57–8:1). All of these men had significant encounters with God after their failings, which led to deep change and transformation in their lives. They show us that no one is beyond hope. If God can take this group and use them for his glory, surely he can do the same for you and me. He is the master at using imperfect men and women to accomplish his good work.

The key, though, is surrender to God and his plan over our own. This is what Peter learned and it's the lesson we need to cling to.

PRACTICE REFLECTION

1. What was praying and repenting like for you? Were you surprised by anything that came up?

2. Did you notice any attacks from the Enemy as you were asking the Lord to reveal your sins?

3. What did you learn about yourself or God through this experience?

LIVING IT OUT

Day 1
Practice: The Local Church

Years ago we went through a season when we couldn't find a church that seemed to be a good fit for us. We were in a part of the country where there weren't a lot of options. We tried a few established churches and even a startup church that was meeting in a living room. Nothing seemed quite right. Perhaps we were being too picky. OK, I'm sure we were being too picky. After weeks of unsuccessful attempts to find the perfect church, we just stopped trying for a while. Sunday after Sunday would come and go. And as the weeks wore on, I started to notice my passion and desire to walk closely with Jesus were also starting to wane.

I discovered through this dry season just how much I needed to be in regular gatherings with God's people. We finally found a place, and even though it wasn't perfect, sacred work happened there. I noticed that singing worship songs alongside other followers of Jesus, even if they weren't my favorite style, deeply encouraged me. I also found that listening to God's Word being preached, even if it wasn't the most engaging message, still taught me truths I needed to hear. I also found a place to serve and new friends to be in community with. All things I needed, more than I knew I did.

Through this season I learned just how important the church is. It is not an optional gathering to take or leave as it suits us, but rather attending a local church is an essential discipleship practice. I also learned that the church is more than just a once-a-week gathering; it is a community that should inform all aspects of our lives. The early church, which was established by Peter and the other apostles just after Jesus left, is a great example of what church should look like. In describing this early church and how it functioned, Acts 2 states:

> "They devoted themselves to the apostles' teaching and to fellowship, to the breaking of bread and to prayer. . . . All the believers were together and had everything in common. They sold property and possessions to give to anyone who had need. Every day they continued to meet together in the temple courts. They broke bread in their homes and ate together with glad and sincere hearts, praising God and enjoying the favor of all the people. And the Lord added to their number daily those who were being saved." (verses 42, 44–47)

This passage paints a beautiful picture of what sacrificial community can and should look like. Notice that these early followers not only learned together but they also ate, prayed, praised, and shared generously with each other. When Jesus left the earth, he knew we would need the support and encouragement of other believers, and so this is one of the reasons why he had Peter establish the church on his behalf.

This week, for our practice, I want to encourage you to take another step forward in your commitment to your local church. To do this, first honestly assess where you are with the local church. If you haven't committed to a local body, then take some steps forward. Make a plan to visit and get connected with a church body, even if it isn't perfect (none of them are). If you are connected to a church, assess your commitment to it. Ask yourself—how is my attending, serving, praying for, and giving to this church? Ask the Lord if he wants you to take another step forward in some way.

Then make a plan to do something this week. If you're struggling to come up with ideas, here are a few to get you started: email a leader at the church and offer to serve this week, set up automated giving through your bank, try out a small group if you aren't already in one, pray intentionally for each staff member (and then maybe even write one or two of them a note letting them know), or invite a few people from your church over to share a simple meal. The ideas are endless, and I believe the Lord will give you a great idea that's perfect for you and the church you are attending (or the one you need to attend). When something comes to mind, try not to overthink it; just make a plan and move forward. Write what you plan to do below.

How will you take a step forward in how you are engaged with the church this week?

Take an intentional step forward this week in
how you are engaged with your local church.

Day 2
Spirit Empowered

Read Acts 2:1–15, 36–41.

This passage gives the details about Peter's first public proclama-
tion of the gospel. But before we get to that, we need to back up a
little so we can get up to speed on where we are in the story. In the
last lesson, we walked through Jesus's post-resurrection interactions with Peter, making special note of the fact that Peter was both
restored in relationship to Jesus and reestablished in his calling.

Forty days after Jesus's resurrection, he gathered his disciples together one last time. They shared a final meal and then
Jesus spoke these parting words over them: "You will receive
power when the Holy Spirit comes upon you. And you will be my
witnesses, telling people about me everywhere—in Jerusalem,
throughout Judea, in Samaria, and to the ends of the earth" (Acts
1:8 NLT). These words were a bit like a road map to help the disciples know Jesus intended them to carry the gospel message from
where they were in Jerusalem to every place on earth. And then,
"after he said this, he was taken up before their very eyes, and a
cloud hid him from their sight" (Acts 1:9).

Jesus's death, resurrection, and ascension were now complete.
Peter's crash course in discipleship training was officially over.
He had roughly three years with Jesus, but I'm sure he wished it
had been longer. However, as we will see, it was more than suffi-
cient. Peter was ready. It was time for Peter to fish for people, feed
God's sheep, and be the rock. It was time for Peter to live into the
calling he had received.

This moment turns the page for Peter. His days of fumbling, failing, and questioning were largely over. That doesn't mean he was perfect; he was still human. But his apprenticeship with Jesus along with the empowering of the Holy Spirit emboldened him to share Jesus with anyone who would listen. Even when the costs were high.

1. What does the text tell us about the people who were gathered? How were they able to hear Peter's words? And who empowered Peter to be able to do this (Acts 2:4)? How did the people respond?

Can we pause for a moment and notice how Peter started his very first sermon? He said, "We aren't drunk." This may be one of my favorite moments in all of Scripture. It makes me laugh every time. Can you imagine if your pastor opened with that next Sunday?

2. Besides enabling Peter's words to be heard in each person's native tongue, what are some other ways the Holy Spirit probably helped Peter preach his first sermon? (See Luke 12:11–12; John 14:26; 1 Corinthians 12:7–11.)

Make no mistake, it was the Holy Spirit who empowered Peter to preach. And it was the Holy Spirit who moved in the hearts of the people to believe. None of these things happened because Peter was simply a gifted communicator. However, this also doesn't mean Peter was just a passive vessel. He also had a critical role to play. He had to be willing to stand up, raise his voice, and start speaking.

3. How do you think Peter felt as he got up and addressed the crowd (for example: do you think he had to overcome any fears or anything from his past to do this)? Thinking back to Jesus and Peter's last one-on-one conversation, how was Peter doing what Jesus called him to do? (See John 21:15–17.)

4. How did Peter wrap up his message (Acts 2:38–39)? Recalling what repentance means (see sidebar and lesson 7 practice), what do you think Peter was inviting them to do by calling them to repent?

Repentance means we recognize where we have been wrong; we turn away from that sin and turn back to God.

• • • • • • •

5. Baptism is an outward sign of our profession of faith in Jesus. Baptism does not save us; only our faith in Jesus saves us (Ephesians 2:8–9). However, we are called to be baptized. Different churches do this in different ways: some baptize babies and some baptize only those old enough to make a profession of faith; some sprinkle people with water and some immerse people in water. Without getting into

a debate on what you believe is the correct way, have you been baptized? If you were baptized as a baby, what does this experience mean to you now? If you weren't a baby when you were baptized, what was this experience like for you? If you haven't been baptized, what holds you back from taking this step?

Three thousand people accepted the message of Jesus and were baptized. Three thousand. That's one effective sermon! And the result of this teaching is more evidence that the Holy Spirit was truly moving. Think of all the barriers of languages, hearts, and even acoustics that had to fall for them to truly hear Peter's words and take action because of them. The only explanation is the Holy Spirit was empowering Peter's words and softening people's hearts.

6. When we become believers, we receive the same Holy Spirit Peter did. Have you ever felt like the Holy Spirit gave you words or reminded you of truths as you were speaking about God to someone? If so, what happened? How did you know it was the Holy Spirit?

The Spirit is sent to live inside all believers the moment they believe. This makes his wisdom and comfort available to us at all times. Some Scripture passages that support this are Romans 8:9; 1 Corinthians 6:19–20 and 12:13; and Ephesians 1:13–14.

PRACTICE REMINDER

Take an intentional step forward this week in
how you are engaged with your local church.

Day 3
Disobedience as Obedience

Read Acts 4:1–4, 18–30.

After the three thousand joined the movement to follow Jesus,
they started meeting together regularly as a new community of
Christ followers. This was the beginning of the church. At this
point, the disciples also seemed to disperse in different directions
as a way to carry the message farther and faster. As we move into
Acts 3, we see Peter and John, who must have formed a team,
head toward the temple for afternoon prayer, where they met a
crippled beggar. The beggar asked for money. Peter looked into
the man's eyes and said, "Silver or gold I do not have, but what
I do have I give you. In the name of Jesus Christ of Nazareth,
walk." The man was healed instantly. He had been born crippled and had never walked before—and now, miraculously, he
could. As you can imagine, he started jumping and praising
God, causing quite the scene. People saw him walking and were
amazed. They rushed toward Peter and John to find out what had
happened.

Peter did what we would expect him to do: He launched into
his second sermon and pointed the crowd toward Jesus as the one
who held ultimate healing.

7. Why did the religious authorities (priests, captain of the
temple guard, and Sadducees) arrest Peter and John? Even
though it seems they interrupted Peter and prevented him

from finishing his teaching, what still happened as a result of his preaching (Acts 4:4)?

I love that God used a half-finished message to bring more people to faith. It's such an encouragement to me to just take the risk to tell people about Jesus. He can and will use our awkward, fumbling words however he wants. God doesn't need perfect, polished, and complete followers—he just needs willing ones.

⚜

The Sanhedrin was made up of rulers, elders, and teachers of the law (Acts 4:5) and acted like the supreme court for Israel, especially regarding religious rulings.

········

8. The next day, the Sanhedrin questioned Peter and John. According to Acts 4:13 what did the Sanhedrin notice about Peter and John? After this questioning, the Sanhedrin sent Peter and John away while conferring on what to do. Ultimately, the Sanhedrin couldn't find any reason to keep the apostles in jail. Read Acts 4:18–21 and then rewrite their conversation in your own words below.

The Sanhedrin:

Peter and John:

The Sanhedrin:

9. Read Romans 13:1–3. What does this passage say about who ultimately establishes governing authorities and how we should respond to them? How do you balance this with Peter's response that he would not do what the Sanhedrin was telling him to do?

10. Today, what are some circumstances when it would be right to disobey those in authority (for example: a boss, a parent, an elected official, etc.)? Have you ever been confronted with this, or do you know of a circumstance where someone has had to make this kind of choice? If so, what happened?

11. According to Acts 4:23–24, what did Peter and John do next? What was the group's response? Why do you think they did this?

As the people prayed, they acknowledged that these things (including the death of Jesus) happened because God's "power and will decided beforehand [that they] should happen" (Acts 4:28). The opposition they were experiencing must have felt oppressive and dangerous, and yet they knew that somehow it was all a part of God's good plan. God would use all of these circumstances to move his gospel truth forward.

12. How did the group ask God to help them respond (Acts 4:29–30)? Where in your life do you need God to enable you to be bold on his behalf (through words or actions)? Take a few minutes to prayerfully fill in the blanks below based on verse 29.

Now Lord, consider _____

_____

_____ (the situation you are facing) and enable me, your servant, to be bold ____

_____

_____

(indicate words or actions; try to be detailed if you can).

Consider transcribing this to a sticky note or note card and place it somewhere you can pray it throughout the week.

Take an intentional step forward this week in
how you are engaged with your local church.

Day 4
No Matter the Cost

Read Acts 5:17–33.

Acts 5:12–16 tells us that the disciples, called apostles in this passage, were healing people and driving out impure spirits. These
acts brought favorable attention to the apostles, and they were
becoming highly regarded throughout the community. Sadly, this
made the Sadducees, a religious group that ruled over the temple,
jealous. So once again, in an effort to stop the momentum of the
movement, the Sadducees had the apostles arrested.

13. According to Acts 5:19 and 23, what did an angel of the
    Lord do for the apostles? How do you think it actually hap-
    pened? What did the angel specifically tell them to do next
    (Acts 5:20)? Why do you think they were given this specific
    directive? How could this be an answer to their prayer that
    we explored in question 12?

The next morning, the Sanhedrin ruling council assembled to hear the Sadducees' complaint and make a ruling on what to do with the apostles. The problem was when they went to retrieve the apostles from jail they were nowhere to be found. I can only imagine the confusion and wonder this must have caused. The guards were standing outside locked doors assuming the prisoners were inside. After all, where else would they be? When the doors were opened, they discovered the apostles were gone. I'm guessing the guards had heard about and possibly even witnessed some of the miracles that had been happening at the hands of the apostles, and now they had firsthand experience of seeing something that could only be explained as miraculous. It's anyone's guess how they responded, but I hope their hearts were not as hard as those of the religious leaders of the day.

14. The apostles were brought from the temple to stand before the Sanhedrin. What was the Sanhedrin's main concern (Acts 5:28)? How did Peter respond (Acts 5:29–32) and how does this echo what he already told them in Acts 4:19–20?

Read Acts 5:33–42.

The members of the ruling counsel were so furious with Peter's reply that they wanted to kill the men. It's understandable that they were upset since they had just told Peter they thought he was determined to make them look guilty for Jesus's death (verse 28). And then Peter clearly stated that they did in fact kill Jesus "by hanging him on a cross" (verse 30). Peter was resolved and wasn't willing to back down, no matter the consequences.

A Pharisee named Gamaliel stepped up and made a persuasive argument that saved the men.

15. According to verses 38–39, what was the crux of Gamaliel's reasoning? While this standard could help us discern if God is working today, it isn't always the best way we can know if something is from God or not. What are some additional ways you can evaluate a movement or teaching to know whether it is from God?

16. Before the disciples were released, what happened to them (verse 40)? Why were they given this punishment (see Acts 4:18)?

Receiving a flogging was not just a slap on the wrist. It was intense. Floggings were usually given with a whip to the bare back and chest of the offender. Tradition, along with Deuteronomy 25:2–3, tells us that they most likely received the maximum allowable lashes, which would have been thirty-nine.

17. How did the disciples respond to their release and flogging? What do you think Peter was thinking and feeling as he

was going through this experience of being on trial and then flogged?

18. Read Peter's later words written in 1 Peter 3:14–18. Make a list of some of the directives/encouragements that Peter gives in this passage.

Have you ever experienced any kind of suffering because of your faith? If so, describe the situation, what you learned through it, and if you would do anything differently if it happened to you today. How does knowing what Peter went through encourage you for the next time you face any kind of suffering because of your faith?

Take an intentional step forward this week in
how you are engaged with your local church.

Day 5
No Looking Back

Roughly ten more years passed before Peter was imprisoned
again. In this instance, King Herod had just killed the disciple
James, the brother of John. This was the first of the eleven faithful disciples who was martyred. Acts 12 tells us that the people applauded King Herod's decision and in trying to win more
approval, Herod seized Peter and intended to kill him too.

However, God was not finished with Peter, so once again,
there was a miraculous prison break. If you have time, read this
story in Acts 12. I love the amazing details in this rescue. For
example, Peter was sleeping so soundly that the angel sent to
rescue him had to thump him to wake him up. Think about that
for a moment. He was almost certainly dying the next day, yet
he was able to rest soundly that night. How could he do this? To
me it speaks of the deep peace Peter had as a result of knowing
he was in God's will.

I also love that the church was praying fervently for his release.
Yet, when Peter was released and he went and knocked on the
door where the church members were meeting, they couldn't
believe it was actually him and decided it must be his angel
instead. They had just been passionately begging God to rescue
Peter, but they didn't believe it would really happen. This detail
is very convicting for me. I wonder how many times I've prayed
fervently for something and then when my prayer is answered, I
don't recognize it as the miracle it is and instead just move on,
happy that the issue has been resolved.

After Peter's Acts 12 release from prison, he moved on to new communities and cities where he shared the gospel and helped plant churches. By doing this he was fulfilling the rest of Acts 1:9—to be a witness for Jesus to the ends of the earth.

From this point on in Scripture, we don't hear much more about Peter. However, we do get to hear from Peter through his two brief letters. As you've already seen through the few verses we have looked at in this lesson, these letters are packed with hints of what Peter learned and desperately wanted other followers of Jesus to know. These two short letters are Peter's powerful last words to us.

As a final summary of Peter's journey, let's look at a few last lessons he leaves in his letters.

"The journey of faith, the path to spiritual wholeness, lies in our increasingly faithful response to the One whose purpose shapes our path, whose grace redeems our detours, whose power liberates us from the crippling bondages of our previous journey, and whose transforming presence meets us at every turn in our road."[1]

—Robert Mulholland Jr.

19. Read 2 Peter 1:12–15. Note that "these things" refers to the truth of who Jesus is and who we are because of our faith in Jesus. What did Peter want to pass on to us through his writings? Why is it helpful to have your memory refreshed? What are some ways you can do this, especially in regard to your discipleship journey?

In Matthew 16:18, the original Greek word Jesus used for Peter was *petros*, which means "a stone." He then states, "On this rock I will build my church." The Greek word for rock is *petra* which means "large rock." This seems to indicate that the church was established on the foundation of Jesus, the large rock, and Peter, as a smaller stone, would be one who would help in this process.

"And I tell you that you are Peter, and on this rock I will build my church, and the gates of Hades will not overcome it."
—Matthew 16:18

20. Peter always knew he would need to pass this calling on. Read 1 Peter 2:4–5 below. Circle the title Peter uses for Jesus. Underline what he calls us. Place a square around what he says we are being built into.

> "As you come to him, the living Stone—rejected by humans but chosen by God and precious to him—you also, like living stones, are being built into a spiritual house to be a holy priesthood." (1 Peter 2:4–5)

21. What do you think Peter meant when he said that we were "being built into a spiritual house"? What do you think he meant by calling us to be a "holy priesthood"? Practically speaking, in what ways can you do these things? How do you see this as an invitation to join Peter in his calling?

22. Read 2 Peter 3:18, which contains some of the last written words we have from Peter. How have you seen Peter grow in both grace and knowledge? What are some practical

ways you can continue growing in both grace and knowledge? How will you do this?

Interestingly, Peter started his letter of 2 Peter with a very similar exhortation by stating, "Grace and peace be yours in abundance through the knowledge of God and of Jesus our Lord" (2 Peter 1:2). These two verses taken together help us see that Peter isn't inviting us to have knowledge for knowledge's sake, but that knowledge should bring about change and action. Our knowledge of who Jesus is, what he has done, and how he invites us to follow should not only bring peace but also help us embrace grace. Real knowledge always leads to action.

23. Take a moment to flip back through this book to remind yourself of all the lessons we learned through Peter in our study. In what ways did you observe Peter living out some of these things?

How is this evidence that Peter experienced real growth and transformation? How does this encourage you?

24. Now take a moment to flip back through your lessons one more time to help you recall all of your takeaways. As you reflect, how have you experienced your own growth and transformation—big or small—through studying the life of Peter?

25. How would you synthesize and summarize your main take-away from studying Peter's discipleship journey?

My main takeaway for studying the life of Peter is:

Peter's story has a rough ending. Remember when Jesus told him, "When you are old you will stretch out your hands, and someone else will dress you and lead you where you do not want to go" (John 21:18)? Traditional accounts passed through the ages tell us that this was exactly what happened. His hands were stretched out as he was crucified. Peter, though, did not want to die in the same way his Lord did; it felt dishonoring to him, so he asked if he could be crucified upside down instead. He was.

Peter truly became a rock. He was faithful to the end.

While it may be hard to hear how Peter, who became such a faithful follower, had his journey end, we know that Peter's hope was not found in this world, but in the world to come. He joyfully followed wherever God led him.

This is the real discipleship lesson Peter has been teaching us all along: A disciple follows Jesus, no matter where and no matter the cost. This is the only journey worth living.

May you find yourself covered in the dust of your Rabbi, just like Peter was.

PRACTICE REFLECTION

1. How did you feel led to take another step forward with your local church? Were you able to do this? If so, describe what happened.

2. Did you learn anything new about yourself or God through this experience? If so, what?

ACKNOWLEDGMENTS

As always, I need to start with the person we've been studying, Peter. I truly cannot wait to meet you in heaven. Thank you for stumbling after Jesus as an example to me and all the other faith stumblers out there. I have learned so much from you and I am a better follower of Jesus because of what you (and the Spirit) have taught me. I know I haven't even scratched the surface of your journey with Jesus, and so I look forward to many more years of learning through you.

I also want to express deep gratitude to the women of Irving Bible Church for studying Peter with me a few years ago. You made this study better in a thousand ways.

Speaking of people who make things better, I'm incredibly grateful to the excellent editing team at Kregel—especially to Janyre and Sarah. You are both so incredibly gifted. Thank you for challenging me to stay on point, write better questions, and use proper punctuation.

Thank you, also, to my people. As you read throughout this study, it's been a challenging season full of big changes for me. I'm so grateful for the small but mighty handful of people who have walked beside me, faithfully cheered me on, and tirelessly prayed. Tim, you are an abundant gift from God to me. Taylor and Billie, my precious girls, thank you for always being proud of your mama. Cheri and Julie, everyone needs friends like you— you are rare and precious.

And, of course, thank you Jesus. You are the only one worth following. I'm so thankful I get to be on this journey with you.

NOTES

Week 1: Called to Follow

1. Eugene H. Peterson, *Leap Over a Wall: Earthy Spirituality for Everyday Christians* (San Francisco: HarperOne, 1998), 24.
2. Timothy Keller, *The Prodigal God* (New York: Penguin Books, 2008), 120.

Week 2: Learning to Follow

1. W. W. Wiersbe, *The Bible Exposition Commentary*, Vol. 1 (Wheaton, IL: Victor Books, 1996), 51.

Week 3: Confessions and Costs

1. Margaret Feinberg, *More Power to You: Declarations to Break Free from Fear and Take Back Your Life* (Grand Rapids: Zondervan, 2020), 7.

Week 4: Are You Listening?

1. Peter Scazzero, *Emotionally Healthy Discipleship* (Grand Rapids: Zondervan Reflective, 2021), 12.
2. Ruth Haley Barton, *Pursuing God's Will Together: A Discernment Practice for Leaders and Groups* (Downers Grove, IL: InterVarsity, 2012), 39.

Week 5: Humble Servant

1. Dane Ortlund, *Gentle and Lowly: The Heart of Christ for Sinners and Sufferers* (Wheaton, IL: Crossway, 2020), 198.
2. M. G. Easton, *Easton's Bible Dictionary* (New York: Harper & Brothers, 1893), https://ref.ly/logosres/eastons?hw=Justification.

Week 6: Missing the Mark

1. Peter Scazzero, *The Emotionally Healthy Leader* (Grand Rapids: Zondervan, 2015), 196.
2. D. A. Carson, *Matthew*. In F. E. Gaebelein (Ed.), *The Expositor's Bible Commentary: Matthew, Mark, Luke* (Grand Rapids: Zondervan, 1984), vol. 8, p. 545.
3. W. W. Wiersbe, *The Bible Exposition Commentary*, Vol. 1 (Wheaton, IL: Victor Books, 1996), 98.
4. C. S. Lewis, *Mere Christianity* (New York: Macmillan, 1952), 112.

Week 7: Repentance and Renewal

1. Emily P. Freeman, *The Next Right Thing: Guided Journal* (Grand Rapids: Revell, 2021), 59.

Week 8: Living It Out

1. M. Robert Mulholland Jr., *Invitation to a Journey: A Road Map for Spiritual Formation*, expanded ed. (Downers Grove, IL: InterVarsity, 2016), 193.

ABOUT THE AUTHOR

Jodie Niznik has served in various roles in vocational ministry for more than twelve years, including Pastor to Women. Her calling and passion is to equip people to take another step in their journey with Jesus. She does this through writing, teaching, and podcasting.

Jodie has an undergraduate degree in broadcast journalism from the University of Colorado and a master's degree in Christian education with an emphasis in women's ministry from Dallas Theological Seminary. She is also the author of *Choose: A Study of Moses for a Life That Matters*; *Crossroads: A Study of Esther and Jonah for Boldly Responding to Your Call*; and *Trust: A Study of Joseph for Persevering Through Life's Challenges*; and the coauthor of *Galatians: Discovering Freedom in Christ Through Daily Practice* with Sue Edwards.

Jodie has been married to Tim for more than twenty-five years. They have two young adult daughters, Taylor and Billie, and a very poorly trained Yorkie-poo. Jodie loves a great adventure, especially in the mountains, and so frequently laments that the Lord has called them to live in hot and flat Dallas. However, she does love the community around her, so this seems to make up for the lack of cool mountain air. She also loves a great cup of coffee, is a pencil snob, and during the pandemic discovered she had a green thumb. You will frequently find her in her office drinking said coffee, staring in awe at her growing plants, or journaling prayers with one of her favorite pencils.

You can connect with Jodie, as well as find her podcast, at JodieNiznik.com.